DECONSTRUCTING
MADONNA

edited by
FRAN LLOYD

Series editor: John Izod, Department of Film and
Media Studies, University of Stirling

B. T. Batsford Ltd, London

Typeset by Servis Filmsetting Ltd, Manchester
and printed by Redwood Books, Trowbridge
for the publishers
B.T. Batsford Ltd
4 Fitzhardinge Street
London W1H 0AH

A CIP catalogue record for this book is available from the British Library.

ISBN 0 7134 7402 5

CONTENTS

Acknowledgements   **6**

Notes on Contributors   **7**

Introduction *Fran Lloyd*   **9**

1 Madonna the Musician   *Andrew Blake*   **17**

2 Blonde Ambition and the American Way
   Andrew O'Hagan   **29**

3 The Changing Images of Madonna   *Fran Lloyd*   **35**

4 Madonna as Trickster   *John Izod*   **49**

5 A Good Time for Women Only   *Beverley Skeggs*   **61**

6 'I always get my Man': Madonna and Dick Tracy
   Richard Reynolds   **74**

7 Telling Tales: Madonna, *Sex* and the British press
   C. Kay Weaver   **80**

8 'SEX: Signed, Sealed, Delivered'   *Margery Metzstein*   **91**

9 Rights and Permissions: SEX, the model and the star
   Sue Wiseman   **99**

Epilogue: Acrostics   *Kathleen McHugh*   **111**

Notes and References   **116**

Further Reading   **126**

Index   **127**

To Patrick Warren

Acknowledgements

I would like to thank my colleagues and friends at Kingston University that have helped make this book possible, especially Catherine McDermott and Ray Mallaney. I am particularly thankful to the Commissioning Editor, Richard Reynolds, who commissioned all the essays and has been a most helpful and interesting person to work with. Finally, I would like to thank the contributors for their co-operation and John Izod, the Series Editor, for his professionalism.

Notes on the Contributors

Andrew Blake lectures in Cultural Studies at the University of East London. He is the author of *The Music Business* (Batsford, 1992). He has considerable experience of the music business from the performer's as well as the critic's and academic's point of view.

John Izod lectures in Film and Media Studies at Stirling University. He is the author, amongst other books, of *The Films of Nicholas Roeg* (Macmillan, 1992), and is series editor for Batsford's Cultural Studies list.

Fran Lloyd lectures in the History of Art and Cultural Theories at Kingston University, Surrey. She is currently engaged in research on contemporary British art.

Kathleen McHugh lectures in the Department of Literatures and Languages, University of California, Riverside.

Andrew O'Hagan is an assistant editor of the *London Review of Books*. In 1993 he wrote and presented a Channel 4 documentary on juvenile crime.

Margery Metzstein lectures in English Literature and Women's Studies at Strathclyde University. She is the author of the forthcoming *Gender and Sexuality* volume in Batsford's Cultural Studies series.

Richard Reynolds is commissioning editor for Batsford's Cultural Studies series. He has lectured and broadcast on the culture and criticism of comic books, and is the author of *Superheroes: A Modern Mythology* (Batsford, 1992).

Beverley Skeggs lectures in the Centre for Women's Studies, Lancaster University. She is author of *Issues in Sociology: The Media* (Nelson, 1992), and numerous articles on ethnography and young women.

C. Kay Weaver is a PhD candidate in the Department of Film and Media Studies at the University of Stirling. A part-time lecturer in Film and Media and in Women's Studies on adult education programmes, she is co-author of *Cameras in the Commons* (Hansard Society, 1990), and *Women Viewing Violence* (BFI, 1992).

Sue Wiseman lectures in English at the University of Kent at Canterbury. She is co-editor of *Women, Writing, History 1640–1740* (Batsford, 1992).

Introduction

Fran Lloyd

Madonna has now been a major media star for a decade. This is a long time in an age of fast moving fashions in music, dance and popular culture. She has not only managed to survive these precarious times in a notoriously fickle entertainment industry, but has consistently maintained a seemingly ever increasing presence. Madonna has become queen of the world of the mass media through music, performance, television, video, film, the press and – most recently – publishing. Even the most determined ignorers of popular culture know who she is. Her name and face appear everywhere. Intertextual references to her abound. She is the sign of fame for the 1990s, the face Americans would most like to see on their paper currency and the name that popularly signals controversy, sex, power and money.

Madonna has also become an intense subject of debate both in the classroom and in print. She has become a studied object in cultural and media studies, in women's studies, and for feminists and other theorists of contemporary society both in America and Britain. Madonna has been heralded as the 'Post-Feminist heroine', a figure of 'empowerment' for females, ethnic minorities, gays and lesbians, a postmodern cultural icon – or, conversely, a perpetuator of patriarchal values, a corrupter of morals, a super bimbo or simply a 'material girl'. This potent and seemingly contradictory mix clearly shows that Madonna's work is perceived by diverse groups and across different cultural sites as touching upon a wide range of social, political and moral issues.

Despite the abundance of writing on Madonna, she has not been the sole subject of a critical study in Britain.[1] This book aims partly to redress this situation and to pose some key questions. Why has Madonna had such presence in the late 1980s and early 1990s? Why has she caused so much controversy across such diverse groupings of races, classes, ages, sexualities and gender? What does this reveal about contemporary popular culture and society, apart from our current fascination with sex and stardom?

Cultural Studies is concerned with the generation and circulation of meanings in society. In this context Madonna is obviously a

'Be disinterested. Not too disinterested, they'll think they're barking up the wrong tree . . .' [*Sex*].

fascinating subject. Meanings are generated first by the star through her diverse 'products': music and lyrics, videos, films, and more recently her book. Secondly, by publicity images and interviews. In the case of Madonna this is complicated because part of her stardom is based on the public knowledge that she controls this image and output in an unprecedented way. Madonna heads her own companies and makes the final decisions on content and publicity. Her 'first' products (the texts) are therefore always mediated by another set of products: her public image or construction of herself. They are all part of her generation of meanings. Both these products then circulate, continually becoming intertwined and overlaid.

We then have the meanings generated by Madonna's audience. Current approaches in cultural studies, particularly in Britain, emphasize that these meanings, which will be partly influenced by both products (Madonna's work and public image) are not passively absorbed by the audience. Instead, according to their position in society – as inscribed by race, age, gender, sexual orientation or class – the diverse audience will negotiate its own meanings in relation to the texts Madonna produces. Given the sheer complexity of this process it isn't surprising that Madonna texts cause such diverse readings!

All these meanings generated by the texts, Madonna's constructions and the audience circulate within our culture – that is, within a particular set of political, economic and social structures. Therefore 'Madonna', the products and her audiences are all further inscribed by the late Capitalist Society in which these meanings are literally made and circulated. Any study of Madonna must consider her interventions and products within both the context of specific group responses and the broader context in which these groups operate. An introductory essay is not the place in which to provide a detailed study of all these contexts (and the many complex debates that surround them), but rather to provide a sufficient critical context for Madonna which the following essays develop.

Both America and Europe are advanced Capitalist societies where consumerism is the basis of the economy. One function of this economy is continually to find and promote new products to sell. This is done by selling 'difference': what makes one product preferable to another. In the world of commodities these differences are often marginal, but advertising has responded by becoming increasingly sophisticated at highlighting both the finer distinctions between the products and between one target audience and another. Madonna operates within the entertainment industry, which is part

Denim – early Madonna.

of this consumer culture. In order to be 'popular' (which her financial success certainly indicates she is), Madonna's products must by definition include this awareness of the diversity of audience.

One of the striking features of the 1980s and the early 1990s is our profound awareness of the complexities of our culture and society. Through the discourses of Marxism and Feminism of the 1970s, the division of society into different groupings according to class and gender was generally acknowledged. By the 1980s these divisions splintered into finer ones which acknowledged race, age, religion, and diverse sexualities. Categories once secure, such as 'woman', now needed defining by class, ethnicity, age and sexuality. This awareness of multiplicity was partially the result of Gay Liberation, The Black Power Movement and Feminism, but was also caused by fundamental changes in society brought about by travel and technology – which were especially evident in the accessible realm of television. Difference now seemed to replace overriding sameness, whether in the world of fashion, music, lifestyle or cultural or political studies.[2] Madonna's work circulates in this world of difference.

Feminism has been particularly instrumental in articulating difference and is an important context for Madonna's work. With the rise of the second wave of Feminism in the 1960s, which advocated equal social and economic rights for women, it became increasingly evident in America and Britain that this would not occur while the female was positioned inferiorly in a predominantly male dominated society (a patriarchal society). Feminism of the 1970s and 1980s was chiefly concerned with uncovering how and why 'women', as opposed to 'men', were positioned in this way. Feminist theory was articulated from a variety of different perspectives – the cultural as well as the political and economic – but these perspectives all shared a critique of patriarchy and a concern with female values.[3] Sometimes this took the form of claiming an 'essential' femaleness that exists despite culture and which is rooted ultimately in biological origins. Alternatively, 'anti-essentialism' sought to show the way the 'female' was constructed in patriarchal culture without accepting that an essential female exists.

Of particular interest to this study of Madonna are the major debates on 'the politics of representation' of the 1970s and 1980s, and specifically those on how the female is constructed and the female body presented – whether in art or the mass media of advertising, magazines or film. These were initially based upon Marxist and Althusserian ideas of hegemonic power (the power of a dominant ideological group in this case white, male patriarchy) and the concern to break free from this oppression by challenging stereotypical representations of class, gender and race in the media.[4] If, as was argued persuasively, the female body was simply a site for male desire, the object for a male gaze that meant power and control, then any depiction of the female body within that society would habitually be appropriated in that way.[5] This led to various feminist strategies to present images of women's bodies that defied the patriarchal norm of the sexual, soft, woman-as-nature construct (the passive, sex object) or the woman as nurturer and provider (mother, wife). These strategies included presentation of hitherto taboo aspects of the female body (menstrual cycles, childbirth), the taking on of masculine 'signs' of power in pose or dress (the suit for example), the parody of the voyeuristic male gaze or sometimes the avoidance of the presentation of the female body totally. As the variety of these approaches suggest, there is an extensive range of feminisms.

By the late 1970s there was also a definite concern with both theorizing and presenting a female subject's, as opposed to a male's, way of viewing the body (the object). Although first developed within feminist film studies – which drew heavily on a variety of psychoanalytical theories – this raised the question of the subject's or viewer's pleasure in looking at or consuming objects, which has become a major debate across a range of disciplines.[6] This questioning of the object and the subject, of pleasure and displeasure, has become combined with other attacks on the very idea of a 'fixed' identity in our age.[7]

If, as previously suggested, one of the key features of our age is the awareness of multiplicity and differences – even within the 'individual' – then a new theory of the subject is required. We are never 'fixed' subjects coming to a 'text' preformed but, as Kaplan explains, 'the reading subject is created (or constructed) in the very act of reading – . . . there is no reader outside of the text'.[8] In other words, according to the kind of text (music, image, word) being read and the context of its reading, our diverse positions – male or female, heterosexual or gay, race, age, politics, occupational interests and so on – will create the 'subject'. It is not that this often contradictory and multiple identity is new but that our culture is aware of it in an unprecedented manner.

This multiplicity and 'de-centring' of the subject is inextricably linked to the so-called postmodern age, where the privileging of one set of values over another has been contested (at least in theory), and previously marginalized groups can now become equally acknowledged. In this context some postmodern Feminists, although aware of the problem of relegating 'woman' to one amongst several intersections that make up the 'individual', do see the possibility of creating a model of society which is outside of the previously perceived binary camps of the male and female.[9] The politics of 'difference' or the currently used concept of the 'decentred' or fluid subject therefore introduce a broader set of co-ordinates which the Madonna controversy again becomes part of.

The 1980s was also the time when the vocabulary and ideas of the postmodern age became part of popular discussions of change within society. Although the political and moral stances taken were diverse, it was generally agreed that Western Capitalist society had changed. It was no longer an 'industrial' but a 'post-industrial' technological society with an unprecedented degree of access to information through computers, satellites and the mass media. It had become a society surfeited by ever-changing images drawn from the cultures of the past and present. This accessibility questioned previous divisions between high and low culture; of originality versus mass production, or of the authentic, unique vision or style against a popularist, often multi-referencing, accessible language. The certitudes of the previous age, the age of modernism, had been eroded. Most theorists interpreted this as a loss of faith in 'truth' or the 'grand narratives' of our culture, a loss of a sense of history and any vision of a future.[10] Some saw the 1968 failed attempt to transform society in Europe and America and, more recently the break up of the Eastern Bloc, as the collapse of any cogent alternative to Capitalism and therefore of any widespread belief in the possibility of change – Capitalism was here to stay by sheer dint of its economic power and its technological control of information. Writers and theorists argued over the term postmodernism, and what the collapse or conscious 'deconstruction' of modernist values or beliefs in progress meant in a society increasingly marked by consumption of products, of unprecedented imagery, of awareness of difference. There was debate concerning how the now 'decentred' subject could survive in this world. The choice now seemed twofold. Either to be carried along by this multi-referencing system of signs of frequent irony, pastiche or parody as (since they were everywhere) there was no resisting them. Or, to attempt consciously to use them as a means of escaping the old binaries and hierarchies of modernism and gaining a 'space of resistance' within the still intact patriarchal and capitalist structure.[11] Madonna is a product of this era; she uses the multiple 'signs' of both past and present moments of our culture and her work automatically circulates in this context as it does for her audiences.

Madonna's career also coincides with a particular historic decade that is marked by the emergence of the 'New Right' and its advocacy of 'traditional family values', both in America and Britain.[12] The liberalism of the 1960s is seen as the source of today's problems and the call for a return to discipline and moral values is evident in legislation on abortion, sexual rights and censorship and the debates centred on the family and education. The tragedy of AIDS has brought sexual practices to the forefront of our cultures. In America in particular it has led to a backlash against the gay community and fierce debates on individual rights of freedom of speech and action versus public protection which have been fuelled by powerful church organizations and a general construction of AIDS as a 'gay disease'. Madonna has become part of these current conflicts through her products, her discourses and her support of certain causes. Madonna's videos, film and book have extended this debate to a potentially broader audience, but also addressed the pressing question of who controls and decides the limits of the 'acceptable' in society and how far these limits are those of the old patriarchy.

In these contexts Madonna is a gauge of our times. She is a postmodernist adolescent now grown to adulthood whose work encapsulates the debates and issues of our times. Madonna picks up the 'signs', acknowledging the differences evident in American society; whether the multi-racial undercurrents or the power relations of heterosexuality, the subcultures of gays, lesbians or transvestites or the fashionable soft porn and sadomasochism of Hollywood.

The essays in this book use differing approaches to explore Madonna 'the star', her wide-ranging work, and its diverse meanings in these different contexts. Some provide an overview of Madonna's work within the music or entertainment industry, while others concentrate on quite specific aspects of her career or the generation of particular meanings in our society. The methods used are deliberately multiple. They range from semiotic readings of the signs employed, the use of current film theories, diverse feminist approaches and different cultural studies methods of deconstructing and understanding the 'subject' within different contexts. All are intended to make the debates that surround Madonna accessible rather than obscure them by dense theoretical writing.

Not surprisingly, no general consensus on Madonna emerges. What this book does demonstrate is how current anxieties in society about identities (sexual or ethnic), about power (personal or political), and about social and moral issues are played out over the site of Madonna. Unlike the 'unique' art object, shown in a 'special' space and viewed by only a relatively small and often socially privileged sector of society, Madonna's work is available for mass consumption limited only by access to a video or music system. Madonna provides us with opportunities to assess our own relationship to these complex issues precisely because of her powerful position of being able to reach a broad, global audience.

These essays are intended to open up these debates rather than close them.

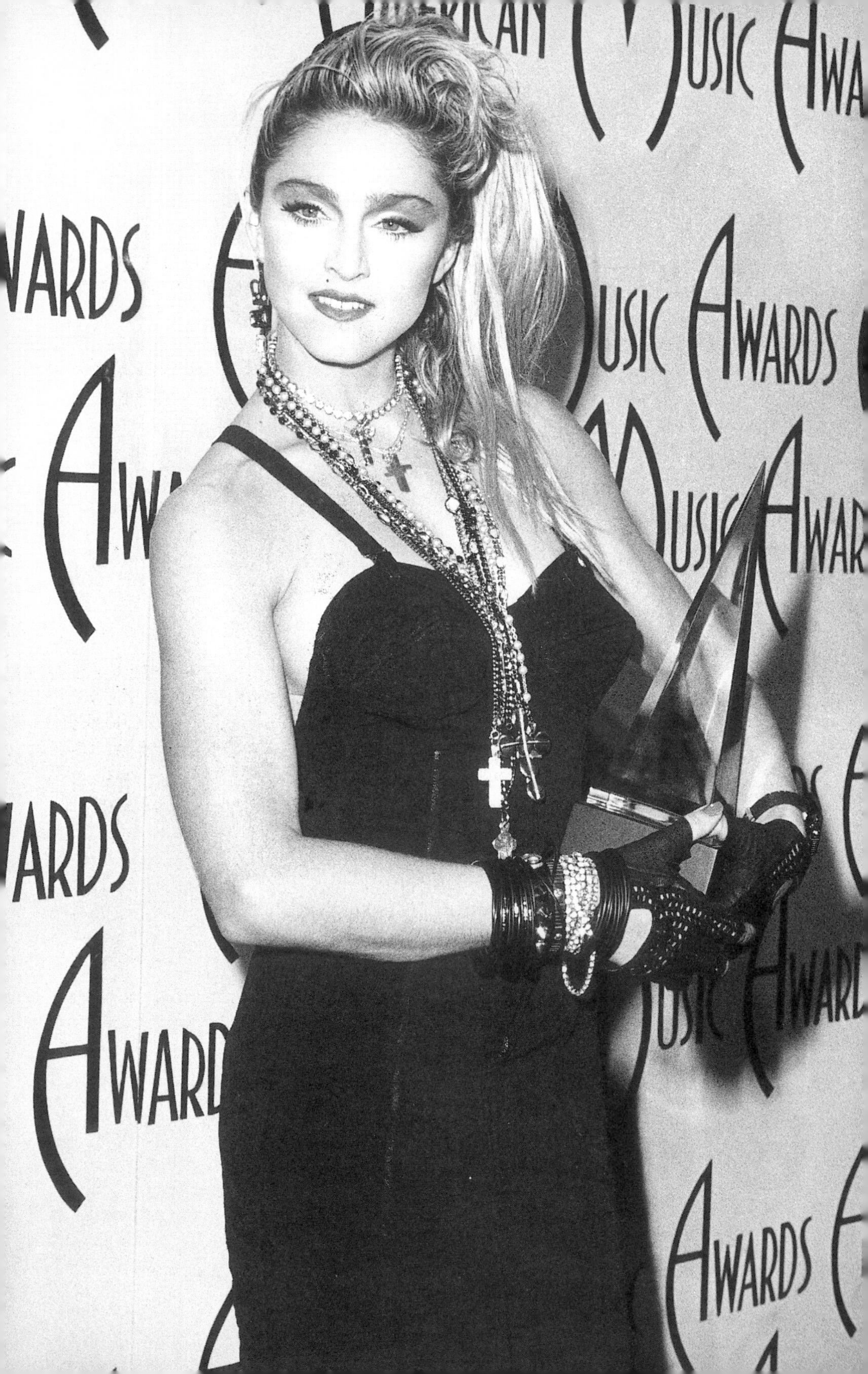
AWARDS

Madonna the Musician

Andrew Blake

Many of Madonna's admirers, in both journalism and the academic world, consider that her musicianship is a relatively unimportant part of the total package. In this account, Madonna is important primarily as image: as woman, as star, as postmodern epicentre of changing shapes, styles and sexualities. I argue here that whatever the merits of Madonna's appearance(s), and her film career, music has been, and remains, the sonic base on which the visual superstructure is built. Further, I argue that this base is not that of a bubblegum pop singer; Madonna's musical career shows the development towards complexity and maturity which is often associated with the world of 'rock' rather than 'pop' musics.

I

Madonna's public career was launched by music. Music videos and tours have been the most important ways in which her career has continued. Yet many people see the icon rather than hear the music.[1] In their attempts to appropriate, deconstruct and reconstruct the Madonna Phenomenon, feminists and postmodernists have, in the main, concerned themselves with the spectacular rather than the sonic. This is in part because the theoretical crutches of cultural studies, the historical, literary, political and psychoanalytical analyses on which it leans, have no developed sense of the musical: music remains an opaque discourse to non-specialist academics, while appearances (and lyrics) are comparatively open to their interpretative gaze.

There may be another, more disturbing reason: the continued inability of our culture to assess female musicality. This form of misogyny works at many levels. One of Madonna's most common collaborators over the years, Patrick Leonard, was missing from the credits of the 1992 album *Erotica*. Leonard's name turned up on another 1992 release, *Amused to Death*, the latest in a series of apocalyptic dirges by erstwhile Pink Floyd bass guitarist Roger Walters. Rumour had it that Leonard was making a career move away from what he considered to be the trivial pop music of

The 1985 MTV awards. The jewelry, the hair and the dress all seem to belong to different dress codes: the effect is pure Madonna.

Madonna, and towards the artistic high ground of the rock 'concept album'. This is a musical form developed in the late 1960s, mainly by male British musicians eager to establish their artistic credentials in a musical culture which overwhelmingly valued the compositional and performance skills of classical music.

In this valuation, implicitly supported by Patrick Leonard, 'rock' is overwhelmingly a (white) male preserve. Male musicians and rock critics have tended to define rock around notions of authenticity and seriousness which exclude music aimed at chart success, and/or aimed principally at young, female audiences. As Madonna is both female and an artist with a long string of Top Ten singles, and as her audience has often been celebrated as primarily female, it is unsurprising to find that her work has seldom received the critical attention reserved for the 'serious' rock musician, and that musicians who have worked for her, as well as critics, have often denigrated her as being merely a pop musician; or have denied her musicality altogether, seeing only the forcefulness of her personality. Nile Rogers claimed after producing the *Like a Virgin* album that Madonna had been the most temperamental artist he had ever worked with.[2] The writer Martin Amis claimed in a review of her career published in a Sunday newspaper, that she had 'an excess of will over talent. Not greatly gifted, not deeply beautiful, Madonna tells America that fame comes from wanting it badly enough'.[3]

This attitude to pop music written and/or performed by women does not exist in a cultural vacuum; it is part of a system of persistent discrimination against cultural products by women or aimed at women as consumers. The romantic novels of the Harlequin or Mills and Boon type, and the domestic soap opera on television, are obvious examples of forms which are quite casually denigrated, treated as trivial, and often ignored altogether. One project of feminist criticism of popular culture has been to habilitate these and related forms as important parts of our culture.[4] There have also been the beginnings of a related move to habilitate popular music by and/or for women, with writings such as Charlotte Greig's *Will You Still Love Me Tomorrow? The Story of Girl Groups in Pop* emphasizing the positive in their accounts of women performers and the culture of the mainly female audiences who followed them.[5]

It's hard to accommodate Madonna either within this model of girl-group pop, or within the tradition of the independent female singer/songwriter (from Joan Baez to Tracey Chapman). Madonna has taken some elements of girl-group pop and its extrovert, outward mode of address to an undifferentiated young female public. She has used aspects of the singer/songwriter's musical control and deeply personal address to a public which is assumed to be aware of both personal and political issues; but she has wrapped all this up with elements from the model of the rock musician. But the undisputed cleverness of some of her songs and arrangements cannot be ascribed simply to the people she has worked with – men like Rogers, Leonard, Jellybean Benitez, and Shepp Pettibone. Any critic who does this is applying a double standard. With the odd exception (e.g. Prince), *all* musicians collaborate with co-writers, arrangers and producers: any undue stress on Madonna's collaborators is part of the general effort to deny the musical authority of the named artist. What is the nature of Madonna's individual musical voice?

2

The question bears directly on one of the most influential approaches to music within Cultural Studies. Despite its heterogeneity, and its naive attempts to celebrate aspects of popular culture for the unconvincing reason that a lot of people like them, Cultural Studies has a problem with music. It is difficult to write about music without taking on the analytical language of the specialist, and thereby alienating the potential audience. There have been some excellent cultural studies of music which face up to this problem; but many cultural critics writing about music, while avoiding musicological jargon, are unable to describe musical processes adequately.[6] Many do not understand music, either practically or analytically, from the inside. This ignorance is perhaps one reason for the wide influence of an essay by the French critic Roland Barthes. In this essay, 'The Grain of the Voice', Barthes discussed two singers.[7] The German Dietrich Fischer-Dieskau uses all his artistry in an attempt to project the meanings of the words he is singing: the lines of the music, and his own physical pleasure in singing, are sacrificed in the cause of clarity of diction. The Swiss singer Panzera, on the other hand, paid very little attention to expressing the meanings of the words he was singing, giving himself over instead to the joys of the physical activity of singing: producing a specific sound, the grain of the voice, which expresses a state of being outside and beyond language. Barthes called this state *jouissance* ('ecstasy') as opposed to mere *plaisir* ('pleasure'). This ecstasy, for Barthes, comprises a more genuine musicianship than Fischer-Dieskau's careful clarity. The grainier the voice, in this account, the more authentic.

This argument about the voice owes much to the French reworking of psychoanalysis, which during the 1980s became almost dogmatic within Anglo-American film and literary theory and feminist criticism.[8] These theories suggest that the learning of language is a crucial part of the process whereby we become gendered subjects (actual men and women living in actual cultures). Since all cultures are patriarchal, dominated by and run in the interests of men, then any activity which stresses words and their meanings can only reinforce patriarchy. Several French feminist writers have suggested that women should and could only express themselves through sounds which owe nothing to patriarchal language. Julia Kristeva, for instance, claimed that the 'symbolic order' of patriarchy, expressed through normal language use, could be subverted through the 'semiotic order' of unorthodox verbal utterance, for instance the poetry of Mallarmé.[9] As with Barthes, the voice's authentic expression is denied where ordinary language is the centre of attention – which rules out most popular music lyrics.

These related forms of essentialist humanism (in other words, ideas about what people really are, about their 'essence' and how they can achieve and express it) remain influential within Cultural Studies. They would seem to deny any attempt to see Madonna's music positively. Even a casual listen to any Madonna album will reveal that there is no single, authentic, 'grainy' voice in play here. In all her records, and to a lesser extent in live performance, Madonna's voice is mediated, processed, distorted, by electronic devices: artificial reverberation and delay effects are added; it is often lightened, even artificially raised in pitch. We may, at times, identify what we think of as 'grain' in Madonna's voice – say on the ballad 'Live to Tell' on the *True Blue* album, or the yearning rap of 'Waiting for You' on *Erotica*; but if so, other tracks on these albums go against that grain – such as 'True Blue' or 'Secret Garden'.

If the lack of a single authentic voice is bad news for Barthesians, the strong implication is that the voice is always at the service of a particular song, especially of a particular set of lyrics – bad news also for the Kristevans. Clearly, Madonna's voice is for the most part deeply implicated in the structures of meaning produced by and within orthodox language. *Jouissance* would, therefore, seem to be the last thing we should expect from a Madonna song. Indeed, by these arguments, Madonna has no voice: patriarchy speaks through her lyrics.

These theoretical positions produce a paradox: how can so many songs about pleasure lack authentic joy? From the relatively naive stress on pleasure of 'Holiday' and 'Where's the Party?' through the S&M games explicitly praised in 'Hanky Panky' and much of the

The rock star attacks the microphone like this, the soul singer seduces it. Madonna can do both.

Erotica album, *jouissance* of one sort or another is actively sought. Even if you insist that the voice cannot express joy through language, there are ways in which Madonna's work reveals a rather more interesting 'grain' than that proposed by Barthes. Grain in wood is, after all, a set of lines which accumulate, with age, around the centre of a tree. Grain signals growth. The grain in Madonna's voice has likewise changed with age. In the first two albums, the emphasis is almost always on the light, 'teenage' voice; thereafter there is an increasing tendency towards thicker and deeper vocal sound. Though this process has been aided and abetted by the technological mediations mentioned above, the overall emphasis is of accretion, growth, maturation – within the constant emphasis in the lyrics on specifically female desires which run counter to patriarchal values of female domesticity and chastity.

I argue, then, that Madonna has a voice: that it has grain, although produced against that of Barthes's essay; and that the voice in its acute expression both of desire and of control over the musical process, has gone at least as far in the subversion of patriarchal values as have the writings of academic feminism. While there is no single, authentic voice, there is throughout Madonna's work a controlling musicality, a musicianship which the rest of this essay will explore.

3

Madonna's albums and singles have charted worldwide, since 1983, consistently. Her world tours have been both aesthetically ambitious and commercially successful. This points to two significant aspects of her musicality. Firstly, to succeed, even the crassest most commercial pop music aimed at teenagers needs constant attention to changing styles and orthodoxies. Madonna has always been aware of this. Each album has been responsive to the immediate musical circumstances of its creation. The *First Album* (1983) took from synthesizer pop and disco music, with an obvious debt on 'Lucky Star', 'Holiday', and 'Physical Attraction' to the disco formula perfected by the Chic organization, and heard on early-80s albums by Chic, Sister Sledge, Deborah Harry, Diana Ross, and perhaps most importantly the *Let's Dance* album by David Bowie (1983). Rhythm guitars opposed in the stereo mix chop over a basic four beats to the bar bass drum, while keyboard instruments provide occasional flourishes or sustained chords. This simple formula, emphasizing repetition and accumulation rather than the linear harmonic progressions of most pop (and most other Western music) makes effective dance music.

Secondly, while Madonna's music is usually contemporary in this sense, it is also informed by aspects of musical history and tradition. Chic-style disco is not the only style on the *First Album*; even here, on an album which is often seen as pure bubblegum pop, Madonna signals debts, which continue throughout her work, to two aspects of specifically female musicianship. 'Borderline', with its echoed chorus voices and its pushing synthesized brass, is clearly influenced by 1960s and 1970s soul, and by the girl-group pop of the Ronettes, the Supremes and many others. 'Burning Up', by contrast, features a choked, distorted guitar pattern and chordal guitar break; the half-spoken vocal intro, and indeed the rest of the vocals, confirm the influence of Chrissie Hynde, the composer and leader of the Pretenders. Madonna's debt to female singers, writers and singer-songwriters is clear from the start.

Both these elements – the resolutely contemporary and the re-working of traditions – are ever-present in Madonna's work. There is constant use of the styles, and of the developing musical technologies, of the moment. The second album, *Like a Virgin* (1984), confirmed the debt to Chic by using the organization's Nile Rogers as producer. Predictably, the production values are higher than on the *First Album*. There is a plethora of delay, reverb and stereo panning effects. More musicians are involved: most of the tracks use live drums; there is even a string section on two tracks. The pumping bass of synthpop and the complementary rhythm guitars and breakdown sections of Chic disco are well to the fore. Again, however, there is more to the album than its contemporary frame. 'Shoo-be-Doo' brings to mind girl-group pop and seventies soul; 'Stay', in a swinging 12/8 rhythm, with its organ chords and multivoice chorus, makes reference to jazz of the early 1960s. 'Love Don't Live Here Anymore' is a cover – of a track by the Motown producer Norman Whitfield, first written for Rose Royce; it's a sophisticated tribute, using aspects of the Whitfield sound (in particular the unison string passages). Here Madonna tries for the first time to encompass the soul ballad singing style, lowering the range of her voice and singing with more physical power than on any previous track. The album *I'm Breathless* (1990) indicates both the range of reference and the increasing confidence with which Madonna attempts it. *I'm Breathless* was released to coincide with the film *Dick Tracy*: what is on offer here is never pure pastiche of the music of the 1920s, but an atmospheric recreation owing something to the appropriate styles and technologies. On 'He's a Man', for instance, a detuned piano, strings chorus, and drums with prominent ride cymbal, are joined by a Hammond organ (a 1940s, not a 1920s instrument) – accompanying Madonna in full, mature voice. 'Cry Baby' features a thinner, girlish voice, and an accompanying girlish chorus, while the muted trombone, tenor sax and clarinet solos provide the appropriate 1920s atmosphere; the only non-twenties sound is a synthesizer providing part of the chordal backing. The pastiche-Cuban 'Going Bananas' has Hammond organ again, with pushing bass, high trumpets, featured solo piano and Madonna's pseudo-Spanish teenvoice. The album also contains three songs by the composer of musicals Stephen Sondheim, whose reputation is such that he was featured 'composer of the week' on the BBC's classical music channel Radio Three in September 1992. Sondheim's clever chord changes and lyrics are themselves often based on pastiche and/or parody, which adds an extra layer of uncertainty to an album of wide contrasts. Madonna performs Sondheim's 'What Can You Lose' in full voice; 'More' with her teenish voice, tongue firmly in cheek, and with great gusto. The most interesting track, 'Now I'm Following You', is in two parts. The first, again in the area of pastiche, offers drums played by brushes, string bass, piano, clarinets and muted brass. Then the record seems to stick, and off we go into part two, with a funky synthesized bass and drums, bigger piano sound, horn section: the same musical material has been transformed into a soul/disco song.

Two other tracks on *I'm Breathless* stray further from the territory of pastiche. 'Hanky Panky' is in the swingbeat style popular at the time (1990): a 12/8 rhythm emphasized by swinging bass and drum patterns, a sparse horn arrangement, and treated piano ride along behind one of Madonna's funniest lyrics. Finally, 'Vogue'. Here we leave the gloss on the 1920s and re-enter the contemporary – for this is part of a short-lived dance craze. And it's a sophisticated production: conga, clap and agogo bells complement a soca-like hihat pattern, with another, synthesized hihat panning round the mix to give weight to the lyric's focus on the absence of personal identity and the time-bending reality of 'stardom'. 'Vogue's' lyric helps to sum up the point: the elements of contemporary and traditional in Madonna's work are not merely juxtaposed: they are also posed, re-interpreted under the control of that focused strength of desire which marks all Madonna's work.

What is also evident in Madonna's output is an increasingly complex intermixing of these elements, signalling growing sophistication in both the singer/songwriter's own musicianship, and in the intended audience for these products. While there is a certain unity to be found on the *First Album* (with its sound-world of synthesizers, guitars and drums, and the use of contemporary dance forms and their girl-group disco progenitors), more complex unities are attempted on the *Like a Prayer* album, released six years after the *First*.

At first listening, this may not be obvious. From the Gothic-Gospel of the title track, through the slow soul funk of 'Keep It Together', the bubblegum of 'Cherish', to the kids' song 'Dear Jessie', the range of influences may seem broad, even eclectic; a collection of songs that Madonna liked, but hardly a unified statement. Listen again, without taking in the lyrics, and the album offers a more coherent set of patterns. 'Like a Prayer' opens with organ and gospel chorus: the propulsive rhythm the track settles into has a lot of country-soul to it, and the vocals and chorus harmonies also offer a country feel; there are echoes of rock guitar, and a timbales solo on the playout introduces a Latin tinge. 'Express Yourself' is part of Madonna's continuing relationship with the soul musics of her youth: the choppy rhythm guitar, Wurlitzer piano chords, mobile bass part and live horn section are all redolent of the soul of the early 1970s.

The next track on *Like a Prayer*, 'Love Song', appears at first hearing to stick out like a sore thumb. 'Love Song' was co-written with Prince, and the Princely signs are there for all to hear: the eccentricity of the drum pattern, the sparseness of the production emphasizing the quirky lyrics and vocal lines, delivered in duet by our heroine and Prince himself. It could be argued that Madonna makes a fair shot at sounding like a standard-issue Prince female vocalist: compare her work here with Cat and Sheila E on the 1988 *Lovesexy* album, or Sheena Easton on 'The Arms of Orion', from the 1989 *Batman* soundtrack. There is, however, another reading: Madonna is here lightening her voice in a way reminiscent of country singers. Country musics are one of the constant influences that bind the materials on *Like a Prayer* together, as the next selection, 'Till Death Do Us Part' illustrates. Again, at first hearing this may come over as an amusing, perhaps lyrically subversive, piece of bubblegum. Simple drums, hihat and energetic guitars provide an infectious rhythm; a bongo drum (Latin percussion again) joins in while the gravelly voice-over leads into a chorus in which the yearning thirds of country music are in evidence; as the track proceeds it is washed over by the sound of steel guitar (the definitive solo instrument in country and western musics), while wah-wah rhythm guitar chops remind us of the country-soul connections.

The country influence is apparent on the ballad 'Promise to Try', where we also hear a nod in the direction of the Lennon-McCartney songwriting team. The bubblegummy 'Cherish' reintroduces the (soul) horn section, and the (country) steel guitar. 'Dear Jessie' looks again towards the Beatles, especially George Martin's arrangements. 'Oh Father' is another country-style ballad, in a swinging 12/8 time, with the sound of the steel guitar, and the yearning vocals, re-echoing sounds, emphases, and harmonies that we hear elsewhere on the album. 'Keep it Together' is another early 1970s soul anthem. 'Pray for Spanish Eyes' brings to the fore the Latin tinge that has been present on many of the percussion tracks. Spanish guitar, castanets and bongos are prominent sounds, with a neat central solo by the guitar; Mexican-style trumpets are heard, while the bass suggests tango rhythms. The album closes with 'Act of Contrition', whose lyrics clearly impact on the rest of the album, but whose music will surprise people who think of Madonna as a pop singer. The music supports the confusion in the lyrics by reversing some of the rhythm and chorus parts of 'Like a Prayer', and then superimposing an aggressive rock guitar solo.

I'm not proposing that *Like a Prayer* offers the lyrical and musical unities of the 'Concept Album', the form valued so highly by Patrick Leonard. Rather, that like this book, it can be seen as a collection of essays with several common reference points: country and soul musics first of all, and secondly Latin musics and the songs of the Beatles. The 1992 album *Erotica* is closer to the 'concept' model, unified both in its subject matter (sex and sexualities) and its sound-world. *Erotica* is very much a product of artist, producer (Shepp Pettibone) and sampler. The sampler is used to provide looped and repeated bass riffs and drum patterns, in this case (as in most dance-related music) taken from old soul records. Drum samples, and drum machine programmes, provide the basic rhythmic accompaniment for all fourteen of *Erotica*'s tracks. The use of up-to-date dance music is as noticeable here as on any previous album. 'Deeper and Deeper' runs away at the sort of tempo associated with Ecstasy (rather than adrenalin) driven heartbeat: its fussy drums and synthesizer lines call to mind the gay discopop of Erasure and others. The reprise of 'Waiting for You', Madonna's reflection on the paradoxes of male and female sexuality, uses macho rap and ragga, delivered by a male voice.

Erotica also uses and builds on tradition. 'Thief of Hearts' and 'Bad Girl' reflect once again on girl-group pop; 'Fever' is another cover of a classic song, this one made famous by Peggy Lee. The country sound is in evidence on 'Rain'; 'This Lifetime' is congruent with 1970s soul. *Erotica* also shows Madonna to be increasingly aware of her own tradition; reference is made to her earlier work. 'Bye Bye Baby', with its speaking-tube vocals reminiscent of the 1920s pastiche of *I'm Breathless*, assumes that 'This is Not a Love Song': music and lyrics also refer back to the title track. 'Deeper and Deeper' makes a direct (musical and lyrical) quotation from 'Vogue'.

It is worth speculating that *Erotica* owes a more subtle debt to the past, a debt to another album about sex, Marvin Gaye's *I Want You* (1974). The relationship is apparent in the careful placing of the accompanying instruments and voices. Throughout the album, as with *I Want You*, sounds are blended in a way which emphasizes the depth of the sound image, using reverberation and level to place the sounds in relation to each other. On the title track the twisted hihat sound meanders away, low in level but flat and lacking reverb, always naggingly present; the orientalized wordless vocalise is given a bath of reverb to emphasize its distance from the more conventional melodies of the rest of the track; and a set of pulsing rhythmic parts, again low in level, zip about the mix in an excess of cross-panning. The final track, 'Secret Garden', is another fine example, its drum sample loop offset by solo piano and soprano sax parts – the piano low in level but lacking reverb and very 'present', the saxophone, by contrast, low in level again but virtually drowned in reverb: giving the effect of the player being in the bathroom next door. Similar subtleties are offered by 'Down Below', and 'Waiting for You' in particular; but the whole album repays careful listening to the balances of the mix.

For anyone looking for a single voice expressing *jouissance*, *Erotica* will present bewilderment. Voices, those we must attribute to Madonna, are alternatively low, high, thin, broad, gravelly, flat, ambient, present, given depth, sampled, delayed, panned and generally reworked as befits particular musical and lyrical moments. And yet this album, above all others Madonna has released so far, shows command of all the technical resources of the recording studio to make a product whose musical unity is as compelling and exhilarating as its theme.

4

To conclude. We have here an impressive body of work, clearly increasing in both aim and complexity as its progenitor has matured. This is not, in other words, the output of a postmodern woman, dancing without history around an absent centre. It is a music which is complicit with both the personal history (maturation) of the musician, and the formal history (in its use of successive styles, of tradition, of covers of classic songs) of the music. I suggested at the beginning of the chapter that one model within which Madonna was working was that of the rock star. Consider the classic example of the development of 'rock' from 'pop': the music of the Beatles from Lennon and McCartney's late teens (1962–4) to the *Abbey Road* album of 1969. The Beatles moved from simple pop aimed squarely at teenage girls to a more complex music aimed principally at adults. Madonna's work clearly, and I suspect consciously, follows this model as she (so far successfully) attempts to keep the audience which enjoyed her music when she and they were young, while also drawing in new generations of younger admirers.[10]

This is a process aimed at by many who entertain teenagers. Few achieve it. Madonna, no doubt to the annoyance of the male rock establishment, can be seen as one who has succeeded in this move and become, very much on her own terms, a 'rock star' – a producer of adult-oriented music. Madonna's live work, in particular, is clearly in the tradition of rock rather than dance or soul music. The stage shows are rock shows, with all the usual paraphernalia of stadium rock: lights and sound equipment by the truckload; flocks of dancers, dozens of supporting singers and musicians; the combination of massive performance area, massive spectacle, massive sound, and massive audience. And above all, the acting, dancing and especially singing Madonna herself. This is worlds away from the intimate world of the disco PA (where performance usually involves mere gyration to a pre-recorded track). Here is not a film star or fashion icon, who makes the occasional record; here is someone whose primary impact is, as it always has been, through the cultural practices of the music business. Madonna is first and foremost a musician, and a musician whom we have to take seriously.

2 Blonde Ambition and the American Way

Andrew O'Hagan

On the day Madonna's *Sex* was published in Britain, an editor at the *Times Literary Supplement* phoned the star's publisher, Secker & Warburg, requesting a review copy of another of their autumn titles: Saul Bellow's *Something to Remember me by*. The publicity assistant at Secker was not best pleased. 'We can't deal with Saul Bellow right now,' she huffed, 'don't you know we're working overtime on the Madonna?'

As a parable of what's happening in the publishing industry this anecdote is almost too delicious to be true. Yet neither the rain-soaked public who formed long queues outside bookshops at midnight on the day of publication, nor the Nobel Laureate himself I imagine, would be much surprised by this sharp display of current priorities in the marketing of modern culture. Dan Franklin, the director of Secker & Warburg, stood over a large crowd of publicists, paparazzi and minor celebrities at the swish launch party earlier in the evening, to say how proud he was to be publishing 'the most famous book in the world'. In the world of books – as one of Muriel Spark's characters[1] was apt to call it – pride is a rare commodity these days. So why all the damp eyes over Madonna's *Sex*? Such pride and such celebration, over the publication of a grossly-written and reckless dish of hype, are as easy to understand – and every bit as grotesque – as the high-kicking euphoria stimulated by Robert Maxwell's buying-over of the New York *Daily News*. When masquerading as noble cultural crusade, big business has something of the chill of death over it.

Academic culture critics, the popular press and pop TV unwittingly collaborated (years before the publishing world got round to it) in promoting Madonna as that singular thing: the innovative artist who sells. The media provide an endless stream of gossip about the 'astronomical' value of her contracts, her alleged promiscuity and the 'shocking' perversity of her videos, song lyrics and speech. And these are precisely the interests of the academics writing about Madonna, most of whom have drawn both on the gossip about her private life and the hype surrounding her public one, and brought these narratives under the microscopes of post-modern theory and feminist discourse. Though the academics invariably decry the behaviour of the media (while the media laugh at the pretensions of professors who teach Madonna as part of cultural studies courses in respectable universities) they are fundamentally together in asserting one point: the unique force of Madonna's ability to persist, in the minds of billions, as an artist who challenges the orthodoxies of sexuality, religion and the American way.

The tendency is to understand Madonna too quickly. To see her as the paradigmatic cultural rebel, surfing over the Republican tidal wave of family values and cutting across the shallow waters of the Clintonista, is to exercise an impatience born of desperate times. These days, when a Democratic President advocates capital punishment and the wife of his Vice-President calls for the banning and censoring of rock records, we might be forgiven, momentarily, for applauding a little too enthusiastically when a star so visible as Madonna drops her knickers and whispers 'Fuck me'. For a second or two, as an author is condemned to death and a black citizen is beaten half to death at the centre of a scrum from the Los Angeles Police Department, we may feel the catholic girl from Pontiac, Michigan is a truly liberating spirit. On consideration, however, we might come to see Madonna's alluring postures – her French-kissing of girls in *Justify My Love*, her undulating before burning crucifixes in *Like A Prayer*, her bottle-fellating in *In Bed With Madonna*, her simulated masturbation and seduction of the clergy, her public nudity and hot profanity – as the expression of a very modern and very Western kind of narcissism. A regular post-punk Holly Golightly, Madonna came into her own in an age when a certain ruthless and obsessive kind of self-invention, flavoured with guile, arrogance and a spot of talent, brought you everything you wanted and where the pictures and noise of you having everything you wanted were in turn brought to everyone else.

If Marilyn Monroe, in the words of Norman Mailer, was 'every man's love affair with America'[2], perhaps Madonna could be seen as every man's love affair with himself. For Madonna skims the surface of American culture, past and present, with the zeal of a Mersey property developer securing a lucrative slice of Manhattan. She riffles through the trunk of America's pop and movie heritage like a half-mad child, covering herself in glory-by-association with stardoms past, all the while dabbing herself with the exotic perfumes of today's multi-ethnic America. In so doing, Madonna brings all good things back to herself (hand-me-down glamour and an air of social concern without the concern); all things being reducible to the sum of her own self-image. She re-makes herself in a time which loves the self-made, and which duly rewards it, if completed satisfactorily.

It is this game, Madonna's bricolage, which so endears her to the

Blonde Madonna; a still from *Who's That Girl?*

fans of post-modernism: for many of them she is the ultimate pop
cultural cross-referencer, painter-by-numbers, bricoleur.[3] It's certainly no fault of Madonna's that she's described in this way. Yet,
with as much certainty, she encourages the misconception that her
use of ethnic style and homoerotic imagery constitute a threat to the
dominant culture. Whether she likes it or not, she *is* the dominant
culture.

However high-mindedly we are entreated to notice the 'subversive' use of horny black priests in the video for *Like A Prayer* (and
the foolish protestations of Christian evangelists were almost
enough to goad anyone into screaming hozanna Madonna), to claim
her as the worthy soothsayer of American minority interests is
patently mad. She was paid five million dollars by Pepsi for her *Like
A Prayer* advert, an advert that would further please her postmodern defenders by being the first one to be 'advertised' in the
weeks running up to its appearance on MTV. They would also
stress that the advertising campaign was banned, due to the
influence of right-wing pressure groups. The banning of the advert
was all-too predictable: throw in a black priest, some Ku Klux Klan
hoods, a fiery cross and a couple of over-erect candlesticks on

prime-time American TV and watch it all happen. Two minutes later, Madonna's single is Number One, she gets to keep the five million and her 'complex' deployment of ugly hoods, fine Gospel singers and love among the candlesticks receives nothing but raves from academics who warm to her 'understanding of the positive elements of African-American culture as well as the negative impact of racism in white America'.[4] The music's formulaic, the message is double-trite and the money's in the account. Radical, right?

Like her appropriation of gay style and feminist attitude, Madonna's questioning of political authority always brings to mind the 'up yours' argot of teen rebellion. In a girl of her age, in her profession, it has the shrill ring of gimmickry. She may indeed drape herself in a Mexican shawl, sing of 'La Isla Bonita', click her Cubans, boast of ass-fucking and tell the black girls in Queens what time it is, but the most overtly political thing Madonna will do is wrap herself in the flag and tell people to vote, though she won't be voting herself. Rock the Vote, maybe, but rock the boat not. For all the confused political phrase-making and giving of the finger to the Establishment, Madonna's songs depend on the slick syncopations of disco and, after all, the message is the same: 'have a good time', 'you can dance', 'it's time to celebrate', 'get into the groove', 'strike a pose, there nuthin' to it' and many such expressions of revolutionary angst. Like her moral cousins, the New Puritans, Madonna is a child of the Reagan era: a New Pioneer. She staked her claim at the very centre of the Me-generation, much like the more visible of her contemporaries and champions on the lecture circuit. By peddling ethnic, feministical and gay ideas to fashion – whilst taking none of the risks and absorbing none of the real flak – Madonna has proved herself the decadent queen of the global leisure market. The establishment takes Madonna's abuse with a knowing smirk, occasionally banning her to her room but admiring her cute tenacity and her Italian-American instinct not to wander too far from the bosom of the protective family. In the places that count, Madonna's about as dangerous as John Denver.

Like the girl in Dorothy Parker's story *The Big Blonde*, Madonna is 'the type that incites some men when they use the word "blonde" to click their tongues and wag their heads roguishly'.[5] She has very cleverly absorbed a number of salient myths, most of them exemplified by the century's better American blondes (Carole Lombard, Marilyn Monroe, Mae West, Andy Warhol), and re-presented them in a style found to be more street-smart (and therefore more sexy) by today's audiences. The substance of Madonna's public persona may reside in such myths – a handful of showbusiness cliches elevated to the dramatic pitch of a Three-Act opera. During *In Bed With Madonna*, we see our blonde at her mother's grave; rolling over on it, kissing the headstone, pressing her face into the top-soil, staring into the middle-distance and (in a voice-over) telling us how wasted she was by the loss of her mother. She confesses that at the age of five it left her 'with an intense longing to fill a sort of emptiness'. Just like Marilyn, who always talked of her career as a sort of revenge on the loneliness she suffered due to her mother's madness and incarceration, Madonna often talks of her struggle to become a star as if it were a long fight against neglect, poverty and isolation. In fact she came from a large, close, upper-middle-class family and, by all accounts, was spoilt rotten.

After winning a dance scholarship to the University of Michigan and dropping out, Madonna went to New York and was soon among friends, rehearsing and making contacts. In her own version, however, she comes off like one of the lachrymose hoofers in *A Chorus Line*: the struggling New York performer par excellence. Searching through bins for uneaten pizza-crusts, hanging around with graffiti hoods, tapping her way down Broadway from one casting couch to the next. This third-rate Vaudevillian schlock – all in modern dress, or undress as the case often is – comes from Madonna as the justification for her toughness and her hard business acumen. We come to see how blonde ambition gains its just deserts, and it's not long before the girl brags of 'manipulating people, that's what I'm good at'.[6]

With this in mind, now look at the way Madonna's biggest academic fan talks about *her* rise up stardom's greasy pole:

> I am the only leading academic who's ever stood on unemployment lines, sat with working-class people in the pits of despair and shared their experiences. Of course, I'm world-famous now, which is fabulous . . . I am the only leading academic who is in contact with Afro-Americans from the ghetto.[7]

Camille Paglia, like her peroxide heroine, is a self-made star fully turned on to the current American zeitgeist. Her baiting of the liberal establishment depends on the same transparent, prolier-than-thou iconoclasm that characterizes Madonna's. At close of day, with sales up and hackles raised, they play into the hands of the corporate Right – who ban them and bolster them and provide the conditions for their flourishing self-love. When 'her mega-self', as Paglia likes to be known, announces that feminists 'cannot see what is for men the eroticism or fun element in rage, especially the wild, infectious delirium of gang rape',[8] how swiftly we recognize the voice. It more than merely resembles that of the author of *Sex*.

In *Hollywood Vs. America: Popular Culture and the War on Traditional Values* Michael Medved deplores the threat posed by rock music to 'property and old-fashioned family pieties'.[9] He also writes of how 'contemporary rock is insulting to the most basic notions of humanity.'[10] Allan Bloom, author of *The Closing of the American Mind*, has stated that 'the rock business has all the moral dignity of drug trafficking.'[11] 'What kind of example should we set?' asks influential right-wing thinker Irving Kristol.[12] Sympathetic politicians have been more than willing to lend an ear to such high-minded cries for censorship. Some have called for a revival of the thirties 'Production Code' (with a view to protecting 'traditional standards of decency'); the National Endowment for the Arts has withdrawn grants from touring exhibitions containing 'irreligious' work; Miami Judge Jose Gonzalez ruled that the recordings of rap group 2 Live Crew were legally obscene; and charges of immorality have been levelled at a whole range of arts and entertainments from *The Simpsons* – a TV cartoon serial – to rock groups REM, Niggers With Attitude and Schooly D, and films such as *The Last Temptation of Christ* and *The Silence of the Lambs*. Judeo-Christian zealots and reactionary politicians have occupied themselves with the task of demonizing all art that threatens cultural orthodoxy and The American Way. This fairly united effort, being made by a variety of political and religious persuasions, was most stunningly summarized by Republican Pat Buchanan, for whom it has become nothing less than 'the battle for the American soul'.[13]

Against this background – where we are led to think of almost any artist as a dangerous radical – many cultural commentators and academics who oppose censorship have reasoned that 'the enemy of my enemy is my friend'. This has allowed them to look on Madonna as a heroic opponent of the American establishment's cultural and political authoritarianism. Following from this, Madonna's champions now demand that we understand her as political activist and cultural demon, as defender of freedom and the polymorphously perverse. In this respect – if in no other – she is a typical American figure of her time. Like Oliver North, like Jim and Tammy Fay Bakker or the deeply Democratic Zoë Baird, the spirit of the age allows her to look like one thing whilst really being another.

Madonna has been blessed by opportunity. She has always reacted against tradition in a way more self-promoting than socially-engaged. Inscribed deep in her public persona are the yearnings of WASP-ish power and affluence and whenever she speaks, whatever she sings, she swells with the pieties of American success. In the face of gross intolerance, she offers highly-marketable small rebellions and arch conceits of a racial and sexual kind. Style over Content, as much as Greed is Good, has been a motto of the Me-generation. In her role as court jester to that generation, Madonna had embodied the full meaning of both.

3 The Changing Images of Madonna

Fran Lloyd

Transgressions or Postmodernist Play?

My interest in Madonna began with her continual shifting of 'identities'. These have received more public attention than her music or dance and yet they are the most consistently changeable aspect of her work. Her 'image' consists of changing 'images' but each new one has a set of particular meanings at the time of its production which then enlarges the overall 'identity' of 'Madonna'. This essay centres on the specific images presented through her own body and the identities that she adopts. The intention is not to uncover a 'real' Madonna but to discover *what* possible meanings these images have and *how* and *why* they have caused such multifarious debates. This involves exploring Madonna's images of sexuality, gender, race and religion within the broader context of the society in which they exist and their meanings are negotiated.

Given the sheer amount of Madonna material, I have chosen to centre on the major, public moments that form her identity and the debates that these give rise to, rather than chronicle her every intervention into this arena. The focus is therefore on Madonna's images on video and performance, with some reference to her construction of herself through interviews and her book. These are, together with Madonna's music, the major source of the generation of her identity. I have deliberately not focused on the minute analysis of audience response to Madonna's work which has been done elsewhere.[1] However, I am not proposing a textual reading of Madonna that concentrates on the controlling force of her work, but rather one that is aware that its meanings are continually negotiated and mediated, both internally by her later work and externally by the audience of a complex society.

The Female as Sex Object

Madonna first attracted public attention by her portrayal of a female sexuality that was seemingly unfettered by any outside constraints.[2] She was overt in her presentation of the female body as an object of desire – the soft, voluptuous body revealed by skimpy clothing, the 'gentlemen prefer blondes' image and the alluring looks and movements consciously inviting the survey of her body – an obvious opposition to the religious icon her birth name invoked. This could have been no more than the traditional female sex object scenario, long part of the music and entertainment world. Instead, it was perceived as different; as a type of female 'resistance' associated with post-punk street style and a new wave of solo female performers and singers. If we take Madonna's early videos there are certain recurrent themes and devices that help clarify the various meanings of this first Madonna 'identity'.

As Schwichtenberg has noted, 'Borderline' (1983), 'Lucky Star' (1983), 'Like a Virgin' (1985) and 'Material Girl' (1985) are all structured around the gaze where Madonna in one way or another is the star.[3] In 'Lucky Star' this is at the simplest level of Madonna dancing and singing, framed only by two male dancers. The camera seeks her out as the surveyed object – pouting, displaying, sometimes at a distance sometimes close to, providing moments of fragmented fetishized limbs and knowing over-the-shoulder glances. Taken on its own, the only things that slightly mitigate this available-for-men image are the odd dress combination of revealing black clothes with the athletic boots and socks (*Flashdance?*) and the star's ever-conscious but occasionally playful jest to the camera.

In 'Borderline', however, the gaze is doubled. The narrative revolves around the dancing street-wise girl spotted by a photographer and transformed into a glossy magazine model. Madonna is surveyed by the camera but also within the video by the photographer. This device highlights the process of 'looking' and of Madonna as the object of that gaze. The narrative emphasizes that she is owned by nobody or more precisely no male; not the young Hispanic boyfriend who tries to stop her modelling or the rich older photographer. Madonna becomes the star model by being the object of the male gaze, but she is in control and independent – she makes the choices. Madonna offers an alternative to the female as the passive object and this becomes a crucial part of her early identity.

In Britain it was 'Like a Virgin' (1984) that really made Madonna a public figure. The lyrics and the visuals construct her image around the old patriarchal virgin/whore dichotomy. The striking alternation of white virginal wedding dress and black sexy number – both adorned by the cross and linked by a defiant, overt sexuality – create a powerful image of Madonna as the brazen object of desire. The absence of a 'partner', the direct playing to the camera and the lyrics make us, the audience, the implied lover. Madonna's control and power is again exerted as a sexualized object and it is difficult not to read this as addressed primarily to a male gaze, even though

Madonna is clearly playing with the stereotypes.

This image of being in control both because of and despite the male gaze becomes more complex in the 'Material Girl' (1985) video. It opens with two men 'watching' an actress (Madonna) on film. The powerful male (director/producer?) is besotted with the star. In the subsequent shots the actress pastiches Marilyn Monroe's 'Diamonds are a Girl's Best Friend' (from *Gentlemen Prefer Blondes*) and sings of her interest only in wealthy men. Off-stage, however, the actress rejects expensive presents, and the besotted male power figure finally 'wins' her with a bunch of daisies and a battered truck. As Ann Kaplan has noted in her study of MTV, the video is full of ambiguities[4] – the sound track of the song completely contradicts the off-stage narrative; it is unclear when we are watching the actress 'live' or on film and all of course are on video anyway! The device of a film-within-a-film based on another film (Monroe's) again highlights 'Madonna as object', in whichever guise of star past or present. We are made aware it is all only an act. However, the film-within-a-film also presents the image of a successful, powerful woman (complete with traditional symbols of fast car and diamonds) who is able to control the powerful male through his obsession with her. This woman ends up uncorrupted by money and success.

There are various readings here: through the right choice Madonna gets everything (love, career and, albeit unwittingly, money); unlike Monroe, the star Madonna pays tribute to, *she* is not a victim and she renders the male gaze ultimately powerless by being in control. Given Madonna's recent rise to stardom with 'Like a Virgin', these meanings were important. The structuring of these videos around the male gaze, which is then denied power, switches control to Madonna – a female power.[5] This power, associated with sexual and economic independence, was certainly being publicized. Firstly, by the many stories of Madonna's private life and the success of the film *Desperately Seeking Susan* (April 1985). Secondly, by the Virgin Tour with its official Madonna merchandize, her formation of Boy Toy Corp and the extravagance of her Hollywood style wedding (16 August 1985).

Madonna's sexualized body is the focus of the gaze in her next video 'Open Your Heart' (1986). In a floor show drawing heavily on the images of decadent Berlin of the 1920s, Madonna parades in a black corset, suspenders and high heels, emphasizing her newly-constructed slimmer and taut body. Indeed, this is the beginning of the next phase of the development of Madonna's body image, where she takes control over the 'natural' female form. Madonna is now the object for a wide range of voyeurs and would-be voyeurs: the

young boy; the young men of various racial and ethnic groupings; the middle-aged and the old. Unlike the earlier videos there is less ambiguity of the setting, less cutting back to another 'Madonna', and we are confronted with her as the embodiment both of the female sex object and traditional porno Queen. The historical referencing to Berlin and what Kaplan calls 'the "carousel" porn parlours, such as proliferate on 42nd street' draw on a knowledge of women as commodity, emphasized here by the men desperate to get their money's worth as the shutters descend.[6] Madonna presents herself as the unashamed commodity. As the object of the male gaze, there is no visual evidence that Madonna can *control* it here – only that at the end – dressed in boyish clothes, she can dance off richer but seemingly unaffected by it with the young boy. But the male gaze is partially subverted by viewing the voyeurs through Madonna's eyes and by the introduction of a lesbian gaze – one voyeur is a woman dressed in Berlin style male dress.

Unsurprizingly, it was the 'Open Your Heart' video that brought Madonna's work to the forefront of current debates on sexuality and female power.[7] In the broader context of the mid eighties and the concerns with sexuality and gender outlined in the introduction, Madonna is an intriguing figure. One can see why for some feminists she became an icon. Her early images highlight male voyeurism, she subverts certain patriarchal views of the female (the passive, gentler sex), and she openly acknowledges a concern with power and control. BUT she keeps some of the accepted signs of femininity and female sexuality intact. A new kind of sexual but liberated woman had arrived who could sport a Boy Toy belt with street style, or combine it with the glossy Hollywood Star image. By commodifying her body and taking control of it, Madonna had claimed sexual and economic power. She was adopted by some as a figure of 'empowerment' for females across a wide class range. No longer did you have to either play the game of weak female or unsex yourself to become successful: being female was a *power* to attract and control men. As Madonna's audiences show, this was a potent image in the 1980s for many young females, especially in a climate where Feminism had become generally associated with prudishness and a high moral tone rather than with physical, female sexuality.[8]

There are problems with this appropriation of Madonna as a street-wise Feminist icon. Although most of her fans are young females, her male heterosexual viewers may enjoy traditional voyeuristic pleasures also. Such a double coding is clearly at work in 'Open Your Heart'. The demeaning portrayal of the male voyeurs in

Before the bodybuilding: on stage, 1985.

the video would not be sufficient to dislocate the habitualized mode of looking at the female body as object. Similarly, the potential transgression of the lesbian voyeur becomes merely an added spice to this dominant gaze. While Madonna may be able to subvert or control the male gaze, she is still using it and aspects of the patriarchal stereotype to which it belongs to gain this power. Madonna works pragmatically within the dominant economic and patriarchal structure – which she playfully subverts but never openly attacks.

Here we have the key to Madonna's success: her work is sufficiently open to various readings that she can appeal to a wide variety of audiences according to which signs one is looking for or what diverse factors create the reader at that moment. It is precisely for this reason that Kaplan could refer to Madonna in 1987 as a 'postmodern feminist'.[9] It is in this postmodern context where Feminism, Marxism and Gay Liberation have questioned modernist structures and certainties that Madonna's images circulate. She can be seen to dismantle some of the codes that patriarchy relies upon (especially inside the tough, 'male' world of the music business) and offer a highly visible and successful image of female power and control. David Tetzlaff argues that this was particularly pertinent in the 1980s where the shift in market forces enabled some 'career' women to become more economically powerful and independent.[10] Madonna embodies this new woman.

Transformed Madonna – The Transgressor

This is the look of the in-control, public Madonna from 1986. Her body has been worked on and liberated from the soft and cuddly into the tauter image more in keeping with the fashion preference and health consciousness sweeping America. The look also inscribes power and control over the 'natural' or given.[11] A *Rolling Stone* cover showed 'The New Madonna' in fifties style and *Vanity Fair* chronicled her metamorphosis into 'Classic Madonna'.[12] The videos and performances emphasize that Madonna can now control her look by becoming whoever she wishes through dress, gesture or change of hair colour. She uses more elaborate settings and controversial themes, and acknowledges a broader view of who makes up society. Those working with Madonna frequently stressed her control of the content and the final products.

The 'Like a Prayer' video, released in March 1989, made race a part of Madonna's *public* identity. The narrative, realized fully by flashbacks, centres on the murder of a young white female by a gang

1987: the new, muscular Madonna

of white males. A black male who goes to her aid is wrongfully arrested. Madonna witnesses the scene and is herself seen by the gang leader. She seeks refuge in a church which contains a black statue behind bars (presumably echoing the arrested black character). She releases the statue which comes to life. In a bizarre shot Madonna picks up a knife and receives the stigmata. The dream sequence which follows caused the most controversy. Consoled by a black choir, Madonna relives the murder, dances before burning crosses and is kissed by a black male who resembles the statue. On waking, Madonna goes to the prison and releases the black prisoner, and all the members of the cast take a stage bow before the final red curtain descends . . .

The readings of this video are diverse. A preferred liberal reading emphasizes equality of the races and gender (underscored by the final linking of hands of the white woman and black man at the end), the unity of the races in the Black church, and a moral comment on the importance of uncovering racial prejudice and stereotypical views in society.[13] The black man is automatically presumed guilty and prejudged unlike the white Madonna who is 'accepted' into the Black church; despite possible repercussions Madonna stands against racism by revealing the 'truth'. In this sense the video touches very powerful historical and topical forces in American culture.

'Like a Prayer' has also been read as a comment on the Black church, where enjoyment of singing and dancing has always been a part of spirituality, and where religious and physical ecstasy have not been strictly segregated. The church as a place of safety, community and guidance is a reflection of its role for many black Americans of the past and present. In this reading the crosses become Ku Klux Klan images which Madonna, unafraid of speaking out for equality, dances through despite her possible martyrdom (represented by the stigmata). The church becomes a place of freedom and protection which allows these choices to be made.

In this construction of Madonna as social commentator, the kiss scene in the dream is more ambiguous. The black male kissing Madonna could perpetuate stereotypical views embedded in American culture: the threatening nature of black male sexuality – frequently cast as both potent but also 'uncontrollable' when confronted with a white woman – and the problematics of such a relationship being eroticized within a church. Although Scott argues that close reading of the video may dispel any such racism, the other meanings are not self-evident against the broader public 'identity' of Madonna as star.[14] While it can be seen as empowering for Afro-Caribbeans and the Black church, simply because they have a strong presence often denied in popular culture, the video can also be read as Madonna appropriating for her own motives a volatile mix of sexuality, race and religion. From the beginning, Madonna's public appearances used the authoritative symbols of the church, the cross, and her name to juxtapose their religious meanings with her own overt sexuality. Race becomes another controversial theme to enhance her presence. After all, it is *Madonna* who unlocks the black presence, and the odd Hollywood ending makes it very clear that this is a show and she's the star.

The video was certainly seen as one of Madonna's many attacks on the Catholic church and considered by some as blasphemous, with its mixture of Madonna's revealing dress, the stigmata and the burning crosses she defiantly dances through. In America this message was sufficiently threatening for Pepsi-Cola to shelve its commercial featuring the song soon after the video was released worldwide.[15]

In the increasingly conservative climate of America, a new Madonna 'identity' was now being created through interviews and certain preferred readings of her texts: namely, Madonna as the upholder of difference, as freedom fighter against racism, inequality and a repressive Catholic Church. This was extended in 'Express Yourself' (1989) to issues of sexuality and gender. The most elaborate and expensive video so far, this is based on Fritz Lang's *Metropolis*. (Madonna reportedly put one million dollars of her own money into it.) The video uses a futuristic setting, and a now blonde Madonna appears overlooking the world and acts as the inciter to freedom for oppressed males, adopting a variety of costumes that question traditional gender division in society. The pinstriped suit with the corset worn over the baggy trousers is accompanied by the monocle – a symbol of male voyeuristic power but also a signifier of lesbianism in the 1920s. (Here, as a direct subversion of Lang and previous patriarchal norms, Madonna gazes at us the audience through it.) She adopts gestures associated with the male from muscle flexing to the famous mock phallus crotch grabbing. Androgynous images also abound. The male bodies appear soft and alluring at times and Madonna's sometimes seems hard and muscular. Gender distinctions habitually used in our culture become insecure. The signs are muddled and the freedom to choose one's sexuality or a role of victor or victim is extended by the infamous shot of Madonna chained to the bed.

The imagery and lyrics of 'Express Yourself' positioned Madonna's work within the current debates on pleasures and difference. The video offers the lesbian, the gay, the bisexual and the heterosexual male or female a place and acknowledges the appeal of S&M as well. It could be seen as the ultimate post-modern blurring of categories between male and female; classic modernist cinema and popular video; the object of the gaze and the gaze itself; the 'real' and the dream – which the fast moving, fragmented narrative makes it difficult to distinguish. But again, although Madonna gives diverse sexualities a space and acknowledges difference which is so crucial, it is still in a narrative that foregrounds her control and her power: 'Pussy rules the world'. After all the masquerading, she keeps her femininity through the sign of the lace, she gets the male (the final embrace scene) and she controls all the gazes through the visual device of her overlaid eyes. She may have challenged phallocentric culture, but she also returns to secure her central position as object of desire and controller – but now, by and for all!

'Justify My Love' (1990) continues this topical investigation of sexuality and gender with Madonna's 'wanderings' first through the corridors and then the rooms of a Paris hotel. The eroticized encounters include her then lover, a former gay porn model (Tony Ward), glimpses of leather-clad males and females, and multi-racial androgynous figures joining Madonna in the bedroom with Ward. This scene in particular presents a range of continually shifting sexualities as Madonna, dressed in a lace corset, embraces Ward and then, when she seems to reject him, becomes along with Ward the object of eroticism for the androgynous figures. Through clever camera shots it becomes difficult at times to distinguish the gender or owner of the body. Is Madonna kissing a male or female? References to S&M, bi-sexuality and homoeroticism abound.

When MTV – Madonna's main public viewing outlet in America – banned the video, it was shown in its entirety on ABC's *Nightline* a few days later, together with a live satellite interview with a soberly-attired Madonna (3 December 1990). Both ABC and Madonna discussed the video in terms of censorship. Madonna emphasized that it did not degrade or harm anyone and commented 'I may be dressing like the traditional bimbo, whatever, but I'm in charge and isn't that what feminism is all about . . . equality for men and women?' The interview publicly made the work part both of the debate on women's position in society and also the current issue affecting all sexualities – the First Amendment of freedom of speech and censorship. This was the time of right-wing Senator Jesse Helms's legislation denying funding to galleries or artists who 'promote, disseminate or reproduce materials considered obscene, including sadomasochism, homoeroticism, the sexual exploitation of children or individuals engaged in sex acts'.[16] The photographer, Robert Mapplethorpe, had recently been the object of an unsuccessful obscenity trial over his images of gay sexuality and sadomasochism while both a stockist of a 2 Live Crew video and a member of the group were being prosecuted for obscenity.[17]

'Justify My Love' was also relevant to the increasing anti-gay backlash fuelled by the AIDS crisis both in England and America. Madonna was well known for her support of AIDS awareness and her advocacy of safe sex. In the *Nightline* interview Madonna pointed out that AIDS was rising at a 'frightening rate in the heterosexual community'. For some gays and lesbians this statement, like the video, was a positive public acknowledgement and one that cut through the association of AIDS with gays.

Madonna's imagery has frequently acknowledged marginalized sexualities, with gay 'coded' figures present in her videos. Her references to past female stars like Monroe, Garland, Dietrich, and Garbo are also important. While they serve her identity as star they are also key icons of the gay community. Just as in the earlier images of Madonna as sex object, the interpretation of these images as empowering transgressions or otherwise depends on how Madonna's 'overall' identity is constructed by the diverse audience and which signs we focus on. Both 'Justify My Love' and 'Vogue' (1990) consciously draw on gay culture. The use of homoerotic imagery and, in 'Vogue', the style of dance and pose which was first developed in the 1960s in gay clubs, can be seen as providing some positive public awareness for this group in an increasingly homophobic America. But on the other hand the 'pose', the dance or the sexuality can be interpreted as just another 'image' circulating within the 'Madonna' quick-change repertoire. 'Voguing' as presented by Madonna becomes simply a 'fashionable' look rather than oppositional and no longer refers to its power based origins in black and Hispanic Harlem.[18]

Similarly with lesbian viewers, Madonna's free play of eroticism and her taking on of specific past signs of lesbianism (the 'butch femme' and the 'femme femme'), may allow them a space but always as part of an ever-changing array of images that is underscored by Madonna – the final object of desire. Although they may be transgressional images of the dominant patriarchal 'norms' of sexuality, gender and race, they become, under the control of Madonna, powerful but playful images precisely because they are inserted into her changing wardrobes of looks and stardom. These images are always mediated by Madonna the star, and are thus removed from their historical or political context.

However, the film *In Bed with Madonna* (1991) generates some new meanings, and several earlier songs are re-contextualized. For example, 'Oh, Father' – initially dealing with a young girl coping with death – reappears in the Blond Ambition Tour and the film in an elaborate church setting. The lyrics and the visuals link the patriarchy of the church, its authority and control with that of Madonna's own father and her need to escape. Furthermore, Madonna connects this rejection of patriarchy with sexual freedom when the previous setting of the crimson boudoir of 'Like a Virgin' (with its spectacle of mock masturbation) is replaced by the church setting. Sitting astride the altar, partially disrobed, Madonna may have been 'exorcising myself of the guilt of the Catholic Church over sex and masturbation' but the image also attacks any form of male authority that attempts to restrict or control female sexuality.[19] The simulated masturbation scene in fact suggests that the male is unnecessary for this all-powerful female.

'Like a Virgin', once framed around Madonna's sexualized body, is now presented, because of official opposition to the actual performance, as a demonstration of Madonna's right to free speech. The open-ended readings of the early Madonna now become part of a preferred reading of her as defender of personal freedoms against a conservative and patriarchal society that does not allow freedom of choice and will not recognize the legitimacy of Madonna's art.

The Controller – The Femme Fatale and Artist

In recent interviews publicizing her book *Sex*, Madonna has stressed her social awareness, her 'mission', and equated this with the role of the artist rather than entertainer: 'I'm an educator – and I do think I'm an artist'.[20] The book's layout and images suggest more an artist's work than a pop star's, drawing on 1920s typography, graffiti art, pop and punk.

Certain images recall the work of contemporary American artists such as Robert Mapplethorpe and Cindy Sherman. The subject matter immediately links the book to another American artist, Jeff Koons. Koons's recent work consists of large silk-screened images and objects presenting himself and his wife, Ilona Staller, in explicit sex poses. Staller is better known as Cicciolina, the porno-erotica star of film and stage performance. Since the first image of 1989, Koons has continuously added to this series called *Made in Heaven* and ensured a heated debate on whether it is art, pornography or kitsch. Coincidentally *The Jeff Koons Handbook*, which includes these images alongside the artist's statements, was also published in October 1992 in the USA and Europe. Thus the content and format of *Sex* places Madonna's work in the centre of the postmodern blurrings of the distinctions between high and low culture, often only predicated on context.[21] *Sex* also raises questions about whether it is art or pornography, and about how the authorship affects the reading of the images both in terms of her identity as an entertainer and the use of her own body. Madonna's freedom of speech has become part of the current debate on artistic and literary freedom.

Madonna is no stranger to the art world from her early New York graffiti days to those now as a collector, celebrity and sponsor of art exhibitions.[22] She has frequently drawn on art images and many of her themes parallel those of contemporary artists: questions of identity, of power and difference and of the body as spectacle or masquerade. These artistic references are a conscious part of both Madonna's current identity and look.

The most striking feature of Madonna's recent image is her use of hyper feminine dress and immaculate make-up that reference both past female stars – often gay icons – but also draw on the seductive but distanced, disengaged look of the art-derived femme fatale. The femme fatale was a possessor of sexual power, autonomous, a devourer and a castrator of the male. Historically, this is a figure first created by men which epitomizes all their anxieties directed at the emergent female of the 1890s. They were irresistibly drawn to her often androgynous sexuality even though she would cause their destruction and death. Part of this power lay in the 'aura' of the femme fatale, a distanced, aloof and mysterious figure where masquerade was all-important precisely because it was 'masking' this unknowable force.

Madonna has frequently played with this image but in recent interviews she has constructed her identity around the female destroyer in both looks and language.[23] The controlled, distanced quality of image and gesture recall the femme fatale look of Marlene Dietrich. The earlier knowing looks to the camera have gone; it all seems more serious, or else the masquerade has become so complete that we no longer know if it is a joke or not. Statements like 'I have the phallus inside my head', and the identification with the Sirens who lure men through their voices and let them destroy themselves through desire – even if partly a jest – is revealing of a new female power to exert control.[24]

Erotica (1992) focuses on this power to entice through the body and sound. The lyrics speak of wanting 'to put you in a trance', while the imagery presents Madonna as the partially masked mistress of ceremonies whose hypnotic power is reinforced by the strobe visuals. The S&M imagery, associated with both pleasure and pain and power and lack of it, also evokes the femme fatale in this fantasy play.

Madonna's 1993 film *Body of Evidence* can also be seen as part of a wave of film noir coming out of Hollywood which re-creates this femme fatale. It is an embodiment of female power in times of threat to both sexes.

Madonna is an astute image creator of a particular historical moment. By adopting numerous identities she is able continually to shift, update and extend her references. The uncertain spaces of our postmodern society become encapsulated in her imagery. These spaces provide pleasure and moments of fantasy empowerment for the diverse audiences discussed, but finally all transgressions, and the politics of difference, race or religion are used as part of Madonna's personal power to entice and keep control.[25] This power fascinates. Her ability to be ever-present in the media through the calculated release of her many products is awe inspiring. Such female power may represent just retribution for the sins of patriarchy past and present, but it is not (as some have claimed) a Utopian vision of a new society, where no one group's power is privileged.[26] Madonna's power is privileged – by her wealth and stardom – which her identities have always made clear. The multiplicity, ambivalence and the controversy of Madonna's images are in the end more important as an indicator of the complexities of the postmodern world and our continual need to negotiate it.

4 Madonna as Trickster[1]

John Izod

If we attempt to categorize Madonna's public personality in terms of the theoretical framework developed in Carl Gustav Jung's analytical psychology, we find it belongs in two large classes of archetypal images. Her stage name registers the first of these obviously in that she projects herself as a type of goddess.[2] The second is the trickster, a figure which Jung found recurring in numerous places including dreams, myths, religious iconography and rituals.

As he observed it, the trickster took many different forms. However, almost all of them were male.[3] Classic Freudian and Jungian theories explicated the psyches of men better than women, whose intellectual and emotional strengths and versatility they severely underestimated.

Although Jung's imperfect attention to the myths of women is being remedied by a number of his American followers, the archetypal figure of the trickster has not attracted much attention in the arenas of feminism. This may well be because its awkward, irritating characteristics, its unpredictable mannerisms and abrupt reversals of behaviour do not even now sit comfortably with the self-images of women as they have evolved in the late twentieth century. The trickster is too erratic, too disruptive to be a welcome companion on women's route to full self-discovery. This article argues, however, that no matter how uncomfortable the trickster's presence, its recognition can be no less empowering for women than men.

Since Jung's ideas are less familiar to most students of cultural studies than those of Freud, it may be helpful to outline what is meant by the concept of an archetypal image. In simple terms, it can be described as a certain kind of symbol found in the dreams, myths and beliefs of large numbers of people. It both arises from and stimulates what Jungians call the collective or transpersonal unconscious. It springs from that level of the psyche that derives from shared human nature, somewhat like the body which, notwithstanding its identifiable uniqueness to each individual, possesses generic features in common with enormous numbers of other people. Jung argued that it followed there are as many archetypes as typical situations in life.[4]

What, then, are the traits of the trickster archetype as Jung discovered it? In common with every other archetypal image that he identified, it embraces the extreme poles of an opposition. To take a rudimentary example, we associate water both with life (because we must drink to survive) and death (it drowns those who fall in it). Such contradictions, in defiance of logic, are an essential feature of the archetypal image. In the case of the trickster archetype, its marked duality consists in its representing simultaneously both the animal and the divine; it is a figure that manages to be both inferior and superior to humanity.

In Europe, the trickster has been seen plainly as a leading player in all those medieval customs in which misrule overturns accepted order. He is present too in folklore, carnival, revels and picaresque tales.[5] Frequently no less grotesque, scurrilous and violent than Punch (one of his numerous manifestations), he may be as unconscious of self as a circus clown, or insinuating as a jester. Significantly, he cannot be tied down: he is a shape shifter, appearing at one moment in one form, only to transmute and make his next entrance in quite another. Such versatility matches his function in running counter to the orientation of the individual's conscious mind. Thus Jung found that in modern life, at the trivial level of personal embarrassment, the trickster disturbs conscious intent with gaffes and faux pas. Or, more distressingly, the same archetype may afflict the person who seems suddenly to be at the mercy of a succession of annoying 'accidents'.[6]

The trickster is not, however, an exclusively negative figure. Virtually every quality Jung attributes to him maps on to the figure of Mercurius (Mercury), who in turn reproduces the character of the classical Hermes. On the dark side, the latter is a god of thieves and cheats, but at the same time he is also, in his role of messenger, a god of revelation.[7] His rooted duality means that he consists of all possible opposites, both material and spiritual. Jung describes him as 'the process by which the lower and material is transformed into the higher and spiritual, and vice versa.' He is potentially both salvific and demonic. Not surprising then that the trickster myth can express a longing for the coming of the saviour.

In psychological terms, the trickster's turning away from stupidity towards a measure of good sense indicates that some calamity has either occurred and been overcome, or has been foreseen, and integrated at a deep level. In other words the image of the trickster (like every other archetype) contains the seed of a conversion into its opposite.[8] Jung (naming this principle *enantiodromia*) identified a tendency for every psychological extreme to contain its own opposite and to run towards it.

As a figure of myth (a mythologem) the significance of the trickster is both wider than but yet linked to the history of any one individual. For in the history of both the individual and the collective, Jung argues, everything depends on the development of consciousness. Here lies the importance of the trickster figure. Its function is to hold an older, less civilized state of consciousness in conscious view. On the surface of things this is unexpected because, as Jung remarks, we might anticipate that with the progressive development of consciousness the older, cruder version would fall away and disappear. In practice the trickster has been actively sustained and promoted by consciousness as a reference point. The confirmation of this lies in the fact that, far from being subject to repression, this mythologem is frequently a figure of fun which has often given widespread social pleasure.

When recollection of the trickster occurs, it is mainly due to the interest which the conscious mind brings to him, recalling him from the darkness. When that happens, an inevitable concomitant is 'the gradual civilizing of a primitive daemonic figure who was originally autonomous and even capable of causing possession.'[9] Conversely, the absence of the figure in social ritual can be sinister in its implications. When this occurs a form of repression has taken place, whereupon the contents secreted in the unconscious gradually gain in dynamic energy so that they eventually force an eruption somewhere in the psyche. If they are brought back to the realm of consciousness, they may constellate once again as an image bearing the characteristics of the trickster. If, however, they are unrecognized (that is, refused by consciousness) they may enforce their return as dangerous shadow images which both individuals and the collective project in ignorance of their true meaning on those whom they take to be their enemies. Present day Europe reveals numerous examples of entire social collectivities projecting such dark shadows 'over the border' onto their neighbours – who in turn project their own deepest shadows back the other way. It is only a matter of time before inner repression becomes social conflict, perhaps even war. If the anarchic activities of the trickster can (in whatever social arena) inhibit the projection by powerful social groups of such daemonic collective psychological energies onto the victims they intuitively seek out for the split-off shadow, then the value of cultivating this mythologem needs no further demonstration.

Madonna's social arena is not (yet) that of international and intercommunal politics. But it is that of sexual politics. And for Jungians no less than Freudians this is a particularly interesting field of human activity because it directly links social and cultural practice (and beyond that, certain features of social policy) to the emotional life both of individuals and the collective. Jungian theory holds that changes in human affairs (whether relating to an individual's selfhood or the dominant social ethos) are led through the experience of emotions. Emotions in their turn may be aroused either by personal circumstances or by images and events that occur whether in the objective or the collectively apprehended world. Inevitably we are talking about an image collectively experienced in discussing an immensely popular star who exerts a fascination, as Madonna has done for many years, which all those feel who both love and hate what they take her to stand for.

No question then but that her public sees her as an archetypal image. Recognizable by their numinosity or magical charge, such figures are usually mysterious symbols the full power of which the conscious mind feels readily enough, but has difficulty in under-standing. This is the case with Madonna's image. The fascination of this type of figure arises directly from the fact that they derive their energy from the archetypes they dress out. For the latter are nothing less than the contents of the collective unconscious, not inherited ideas, but inherited modes of psychic functioning. Until activated, they are forms without content; when activated their power is so great that they govern patterns of behaviour. Thus they are the centres of energy around which ideas, images, affects and myths cohere.

Jung demonstrated that every individual experiences the grip of a variety of archetypes in the course of a lifetime. However, as has already been said, he proved most adept at elaborating the arche-types that govern the lives and psyches of men. In an attempt to redress the balance, feminist Jungians have in recent years worked at identifying archetypal images that inform the lives of women. In the process, while building on the work of sympathetic archaeo-mytho-logists such as Marija Gimbutas, they returned to European pre-history and discovered that the dominance of male gods both in the Christian pantheon and in several of the world's most powerful faiths has not been the timeless phenomenon the faiths themselves declare. On the contrary, long before the accession of the male gods the peoples of Old Europe worshipped the Great Goddess, and the male principle had little if any place in their belief system. The gifts of life and death, feast and famine were all in the hands of the Goddess. The symbols of her energy included chevrons, vulvae, snakes, spirals, sprouting seeds and shoots; and images of warfare were strikingly absent from art centred on her.[10]

All this changed with the invasion of cattle-herding Indo-Euro-pean tribes who overran Europe between 3500 and 2500 B.C. They imposed their patriarchal culture and bellicose male gods on the conquered people. Yet as Gimbutas and Jean Shinoda Bolen show, the Great Goddess did not disappear without trace. She became the subservient consort of the invaders' gods, and most of the attributes or power that originally belonged to her were given to a male deity. Other attributes were split across less powerful goddesses. In this way many of her symbols were subsumed into the new patriarchal mythologies. For example, the Birth Giver and the Earth Mother aspects of the Goddess eventually fused with the Virgin Mary. Meanwhile her negative aspects, formerly expressed in her function as the Mother who regenerates life from death, also split off. They became attached to the many women who learned the occult secrets of the Goddess and kept them alive.[11] Thus the satanic witch hunts organized by the Catholic Church in the fifteenth to eighteenth centuries (during which more than eight million women were murdered) can be seen as a consequence of an unbridled collective shadow projection by followers of a faith dominated by a male god. We may guess that, driven by fear of the dethroned Goddess's continuing potency, they projected negative archetypal images upon women whom they believed to be her devotees, then sought to extirpate their demons by killing those whom they had caused to bear them.[12] To judge by letters to the press, Madonna carries the projected shadow of many (both male and female) who loathe her, her image is for some people malevolent enough that her trickster is tainted with the witch's darkness.

Long before the Christian era however, the attributes, symbols and power formerly belonging to the Great Goddess had been divided among a number of powerful Greek goddesses and their Roman successors; and it is these figures who have been recalled to the service of Jungian analysis. Bolen, for instance, has picked out seven classical goddesses who form a pantheon of archetypal images derived from the Great Goddess. On the basis of her observations as a practising analyst she argues that (whether singly or more typically clustered in groups) they represent the influence exerted by archetypes governing the lives of women.

Even a cursory look at the seven deities reveals that most of them do not bear at all on Madonna's image. First, she in no way represents Demeter (Ceres to the Romans) who was goddess of motherhood and fertility. Sex in her routines has nothing to do with procreation.

Second, she is not the child of Demeter, Persephone (the Roman Proserpina) who, in Bolen's opinion, has two dominant aspects. In one she is the Kore, the nameless maiden who does not yet know who she is, the mother's daughter, a child-woman whose sexuality is unawakened. She wears her other aspect as Queen of the Underworld, as the guide for those who visit that place. Where Persephone rules a woman may have reluctant access to her own unconscious, and may have the power to escort other women into the mysteries of their own dark realms. Clearly her first aspect does not match Madonna's public persona. But neither does the second, for although Madonna also mediates between the unconscious and conscious worlds, she is not like Persephone a psychological captive, the quality that enables her to help depressive women.[13]

Third comes Hera (or Juno), goddess of marriage. She too is not an archetype to fit Madonna, despite the latter's celebrated marital adventures. For Hera embodies an attitude to marriage much in harmony with patriarchal values. This archetype represents a woman's overwhelming desire to be a wife; she does not feel truly alive until she has a husband, and all other activities, such as career or motherhood, come second to the securing and holding of a man.[14]

The fourth goddess is also completely foreign to Madonna. Hestia (whom the Romans did not represent as a human figure, but as Vesta, a flame) was goddess of the hearth. Bolen describes her as the archetype active in women who find housekeeping a meaningful activity and who through tending to chores discover inner peace and a centring activity equivalent to meditation. Her detachment shields her from the battering of external experience, and her devotion to the inner life gives her the qualities of the wise woman.[15] She is like an inverted image of the singer.

When we turn to the fifth goddess, Athena (Minerva to the Romans), we meet the first of the archetypal figures who govern Madonna. As goddess of wisdom, Athena was known for her winning skill as a strategist, detached even in the heat of battle and able to plan with clear foresight. Ruled by the head, the woman led by the Athena archetype works to make something of herself: 'The equivalent of a female Horatio Alger is almost always an Athena woman.'[16] Madonna, who has been described as just such an all-American, rags-to-riches heroine, is celebrated for planning her career, polishing her image and relentlessly producing herself as a commodity.[17] It is perhaps her one universally agreed claim to fame.

In addition to these strong resemblances, however, there are equally distinctive mismatches. Bolen observes that the Athena woman shows a tendency to do everything in moderation and to live within the Golden Mean. Indeed she lives in her mind and is often out of touch with her body; typically she is neither sensual nor sexy.[18]

Resemblances between Madonna and the sixth goddess, Artemis (later Diana) queen of the hunt, are not as strong, but nonetheless exist. Plainly the goddess's virginity and immunity to falling in love have no meaning for the star; but they share the focused intensity and perseverance that Bolen itemizes as Artemis's other dominant characteristics. They endow her with the ability to aim and hit the target no matter what the distractions. And there is another important connection with Madonna's public image in that (like today's Artemis women) she treats sex as a recreational sport or a physical experience rather than an expression of emotional intimacy or commitment.[19]

In this important detail, then, Madonna's sexual behaviour differs from what might be expected of a woman under the influence of Aphrodite, the seventh and most potent goddess in Bolen's pantheon, who 'governs women's enjoyment of love and beauty, sexuality and sensuality.' Like Aphrodite, Madonna has potent sex appeal and falls in love easily; she also displays every sign of being overwhelmed by sudden eroticism. But unlike the goddess she does not represent the drive to procreate; nor does she seem to want to become involved to the point of merging with her partner, but rather, Artemis-like, expresses an interest in enjoying the physical experience.

Both Aphrodite and Madonna are tremendous forces for change; and this connects not only with their sexual but also their artistic fertility. Bolen argues that creative work springs from an intense and passionate involvement almost like that with a lover, as the artist interacts with the 'other' to bring something new into being. But while dedication to her work makes Madonna a true Aphrodite woman, there is a significant difference. Women ruled by this goddess tend to live in the immediate present, taking life as if it were no more than a sensory experience and there were no future consequences to their actions.[20] In this respect as we have seen, Madonna, a clever strategist, is much closer to Athena.

Thus the two virgin goddesses Athena and Artemis, together with the goddess of love Aphrodite, furnish archetypal images that frame and energize a number of elements of Madonna's public personality. But they do not account for the entire personality for two reasons. First, she is a shape-shifter, only constant like the virgin goddesses in her certainty of aim and command of strategy. Second, her performances, despite her passionate commitment to them noted above, often lack the resonance of lived emotional experience: Madonna seems not to be celebrating love and sexuality in their own right so much as playing with the idea of them, even while she is making them the one constant theme wound through her countless metamorphoses.

Many commentators have noticed these qualities. For example, E. Deidre Pribram and David Tetzlaff concur in labelling her a chameleon of appearances who refuses all fixed meanings. Behind the postmodern play with masks there is no authentic Madonna, no personal or inspirational centre to the vision.[21] Tetzlaff calls her the Teflon idol.

> Nothing sticks to her. The sleaze, the blasphemy, the perversity all slide off. Perhaps the audience recognizes that Madonna only inhabits these positions as if she were modelling a collection of fashions . . . unaffected for having worn them for a while. This is represented in the videos themselves, which always end with Madonna seemingly unfazed by the cultures and struggles she has encountered, dancing off screen to the perky disco bounce.[22]

As these remarks hint, Madonna has something in common with the male trickster both in shape shifting and sexual ambivalence. The shapes and roles she has chosen to perform and then discarded are extraordinarily diverse. We can add to them the roles that her fans and critics have discovered in her acts, through either wish fulfilment or revulsion playing upon deliberately ambiguous film editing. Earlier personae included the Boy Toy and the Bitch. Later on in the music videos 'Justify My Love' and 'Express Yourself' her sexual roles were seen as those of a heterosexual partner, lover of a gay man, of an androgynous man/woman, and of a lesbian; she also dallies with masochism and sadism, and plays at group sex. Then, in her stage rendering of 'Like a Virgin' for *In Bed With Madonna (Truth or Dare)*, she simulates masturbation. Back stage she entertains her dancers by mock-fellating a bottle and hinting that she might be a gay male, claiming that the sight of two men kissing gives her a hard-on.

No question then but she plays to the lesbian and gay audience. Just as some feminists have tried to recruit her uninhibited sexuality to support their gender politics, so some lesbians and gays have sought to appropriate her rich sexual ambiguity to back gay activism. On the surface of things they have a good case, since her deployment of artifice, glamour and multiplicity appeal to them as something familiar, because they too must use such devices to pass in straight society.[23] An important aspect of this is Madonna's alternation between masquerade (burlesquing feminine norms through excess) and drag (as a performance of gender reversal).[24] In fact Pribram observes how in 'Express Yourself' Madonna's clothing (a combination of male business suit and female corset) refers to both genders simultaneously.[25]

In practice her long parade of grotesques makes it impossible to enlist Madonna's image in support of any single cause. It is always ambiguous, if for no other reason than that which Tetzlaff notes, the routine commercial recognition that the straight audience is many times larger than the gay one.

> It is simply wishful thinking to imagine that anyone who comes up with a good old-fashioned sexist interpretation of these texts is mis-reading them. Madonna and her creative cohorts are not stupid ... After all, the media industry is still controlled by men, and men compose a large part of the mass market.[26]

Despite this adeptness and her multiple transformations, Madonna is in control of her image, not trapped by it. Indeed 'control' and 'power' are terms used repeatedly in connection with her. As Susan Bordo observes, they accumulate to give a sense that the star is self-created.[27] But this is also a characteristic of archetypes. Not only can they draw the lives of individuals and communities into new channels, but they are autonomous. In other words, they charge images with an energy which gives them what appears to be an independent existence of their own. Of no archetype is this more true than the trickster.

Madonna's presentations appeal to (or repel) many different sorts of people in many different ways, but perhaps the one common thread that most of her fans and critics feel tugging at them is that spun from sex and power – the power of seduction, the seduction of power. We said earlier that the trickster simultaneously represents the animal and the divine in humanity. In societies like those of the Western world in which sexuality is given high priority and orga-nized religion depreciated, entry into no other sphere of activity than sex is so much desired. No other channel for desire offers so many people the gratifying illusion of power. They seem to sense that through its ecstasies sex might let them breach the limits of the body to touch immortality. Power seems even to many of the pow-erless to be within reach here.

Of course the search for power tends to corrupt no matter where it is found; and for every sexual relationship that empowers its partners, delivering them to ecstasy, there are others dogged by misery. Far from being a romantic, lyric or even comfortable figure, the trickster invariably presents us with an awkward, uncomfortable personality as well as a persuasive and amusing prankster and sex-ual polymorph. This is all the more significant when we realize that Jung saw the divine as profoundly ambivalent, so that in his psy-chology the sexual linking of animal and divine, conscious and unconscious can equally well be positive or negative, blessed or cursed.

What then does the wide appeal of Madonna's image signify? The emergence of a female trickster in the person of Madonna fits well with the enhanced standing of women – the trickster masked in a star persona confirms that she is not to be taken as pliable. A creature of infinite variety, she bends only to her own whim, not to the fancy of man. Perhaps there is some kind of role model for young women here; however, it is worth suggesting that a model who offers so much parodic sex with so little emotion is not in the longer term a positive one.

We should therefore go further than this. Jung's writings lament the way in which twentieth-century Western humanity continues to bring many of its worst pains upon itself. Complacent in the know-ledge of advances in human consciousness which science and tech-nology daily confirm, civilized people undervalue the unconscious. Whether we forget it, repress it, or devalue it by ridiculing an interest in the activity of the unconscious as superstition, we cut ourselves off from it at our peril, he argued. The trickster keeps an older state of consciousness in our minds. The rambunctious and downright irritating nature of this mythologem's presence reminds us, however, that among the other characteristics of earlier states of consciousness was an openness to the kinds of intrusion of uncons-cious impulses that the trickster herself represents.

One strand of imagery that Madonna favours, and which supplies recurring parodic references to Catholicism, is the icons such as crosses, the stigmata she receives on her hands in the video 'Like a Prayer', and (more insistently than anything else) her name. She pulls all these images out of their normal context and relocates them centrally in her ceremonies of sex. We can of course say with E. Ann Kaplan that, with the aid of these religious icons, Madonna con-structs a thinly disguised autobiographical account of her rebellion against a repressive Catholic upbringing; and we can agree that such an adolescent story may well appeal to some of her fans.[28] But it is questionable whether the subversion of sexual repression accounts for the Madonna phenomenon in its entirety.

From the Jungian point of view, the intrusion of Catholic icons into Madonna's celebrations of sexuality brings into play an all but moribund set of images. They now express a dogma that has lost its spiritual and emotional excitement, and which for most people in Western culture has no vitality. Reintroducing these icons suits well Madonna's task as trickster because it recalls to mind an older state of consciousness involved in the observance of organized religious practice and the formal approach to the unconscious. So Madonna as trickster draws the old ways back to mind, but in the absence of an effective organized religion places them in the setting of another fundamental human activity. Her performances proffer sexually electrified images to supply the charge by which those of her fans who (in whatever confusion or uncertainty) sense the need for self-knowledge, may be stimulated into beginning to feel their way, so to speak, towards that inner goal. It is entirely to the point that, as it confronts our conscious selves with urgent drives and dream images that arise out of the unconscious, sex, like religion, causes us both pleasure and pain, and forces us to experience more fully both the light and the dark, promising both ecstasy and despair.

All this may seem to prepare the way for grandiose claims of describing Madonna as a priestess. Finally, it does not. The priestess serves organized religion and obeys a pre-existent doctrine which she ministers to the faithful. She must by definition be conscious that she is following the practices of her predecessors in her rituals, while mediating between the gods and humans, between the unconscious and the conscious. Madonna may or may not be aware of what she is doing in sponsoring this kind of mediation; but she is by no means observing a doctrine.

As a trickster, however, she has something of the shaman about her. This figure, an unconscious healer, also sometimes plays tricks on people, inflicting discomfort on them (which may well rebound upon him- or herself) in the process of breaking through to and healing the psyche.[29] For the shaman is, as Maggy Anthony says, one who works by intuition and seeks a way alone, unaided and one step at a time, through the wilderness of the human condition to discover who the gods are and what they say.[30] It is not necessary to pretend that Madonna consciously practises such powers or has special insight into the human unconscious. But nonetheless the emotional decentering caused by the force of her performances gives her imagery the catalytic power shared by trickster and shaman. Thus it stirs ancient passions and symbols in the collective unconscious of those people within her audiences in whom the appetite for the inner journey is awakening. This may occur for men as well as women, but it remains true that the female trickster has an especial importance for women.

The tricksters and jesters of the past were almost always male. Previously they rather than women could violate society's norms, acting the awkward prankster, behaving unpredictably or even in a downright malevolent way, and get away with it. But women who did so would have risked being excoriated and labelled as witches. It is significant that, no matter how much Madonna has aroused anger and vilification, she has (occasional short-term bannings of videos aside) neither been silenced nor pilloried. She has not suffered the witch's fate. On the contrary, in playing the trickster she has empowered herself, and now the archetype she has activated is available to help other women take the power they need.

5 A Good Time For Women Only

Beverley Skeggs

'I only have to be rebellious because others are so reactionary'
(30 December 1992)[1]

Madonna deals with sexuality, she plays with its boundaries. She exposes the power relations implicit in sexuality and in so doing challenges the traditional definitions which silence the expression of sexuality by women and by those who do not conform to the institutionalized definitions of sexuality. We need to remember, rather than being an intimate and personal expression, sexuality is one of the most legislated forms of social expression. Legislation such as marriage, tax and social security systems make sure that those who do not conform do not reap any social benefits. In the UK, legislation such as Clause 28 and the Educational Reform Act inhibit the expression of any form of sexuality other than heterosexual. Medical and moral propaganda continually inform us of the boundaries of normality by identifying and classifying that which is deviant. And the legal system exists to make sure the boundaries of normality remain intact. Plentiful cultural materials are produced to extol the myth of the romantic heterosexual couple and the family as a safe haven from a heartless world (the fact that most abuse of women and children takes place in the family structure is rarely mentioned alongside these myths).

Speaking of sexuality is sometimes dismissed as being a privilege of those with opulent Western lifestyles, yet we need to remember that sexuality is one of the most fundamental forms of other and self-regulation which takes specifically gendered forms. The expression of women's sexuality is highly regulated by both internal and external mechanisms. Historically, we can see a long hegemonic battle by which various powerful groups of men have been able to consolidate their power, using their access to economics and the state, to silence women. Elias[2] notes how the control of sexual expression was a central feature of the civilisation process of Western society. The ethnographies of Sue Lees,[3] Chris Griffin[4] and myself show only too clearly how young women learn to police themselves and others through the fear of, or articulation of, the term 'slag'. Madonna rejects the self-monitoring of female sexuality.

'Express Yourself.'

She transgresses the boundaries of containment that most women *have* to conform to in order not to be culturally ostracized or forfeit any future economic rewards.

Madonna works with what she knows at the level of sexual politics. Firstly through her position as Catholic female, challenging restrictions on the expressions of female sexuality, and secondly through her close links to the lesbian and gay communities in New York who, for years, have advocated the celebration of their sexuality in the face of increasing controls and danger. Madonna has done a great deal of work for HIV/AIDS support groups. The track 'In This Life' on the album *Erotica* describes the pain of friends dying and the frustration with the ignorance and uncaring attitudes that surround us: 'Ignorance is not Bliss' states Madonna.

The Gaze and Sexuality

Popular music is the perfect vehicle for enabling challenges to sexual constraints. Sex sells music. While both the sounds and the visuals encode different forms of sexuality, I will concentrate on the visuals (John Shepherd[5] and Susan McClary[6] provide analyses of sound and gender).

One regular representation of women in popular music is of vulnerability and availability. Women such as Kylie Minogue, Witney Houston and Belinda Carlisle represent femininity; they are dressed in clothes which whilst displaying their body work at the level of suggestiveness rather than explicitness. These women appear as projections of masculine fantasy. They are what some men would like women to be.

Catherine McKinnon,[7] taking up a non-psychoanalytical reading of Laura Mulvey's work argues that the gaze is always constructed as male. This gives men the permission, ability and the power to look at women, rendering women as objects for male pleasure. In pornography, McKinnon argues, it is the gaze that eroticizes the despised, the demeaned, the accessible, the there-to-be-used, the servile, the childlike, the passive and the animal. She argues that sexual desire is constructed in such a way that we (as women) come to want our own self-annihilation. Sheila Jeffreys[8] takes a similar position, arguing that women gain pleasure from the process of eroticizing our degradation.

I want to take issue with these accounts. In them I cannot find any space for the construction of meaningful female sexuality. They suggest that women can never be free from conspiratorial male manipulation. Any form of resistance or opposition is trapped within male domination. This also leads us into a form of essentialism where we assume that women are naturally socially different to men. Ellen Willis[9] argues that male power and female powerlessness are not absolute categories. If we read them as such, we are unable to perceive scope for change, resistance or struggle. We also reproduce the dichotomy of heterosexuality. If sexuality and desire are simply seen as functions of an all-pervasive male power there can, by definition, be no meaningful female sexuality. Stacey[10] suggests that if we argue that women are different from men in their relation to visual constructions of femininity, then we have to ask: do all women have the same relationship to images of themselves? Is there only one spectator position? How do we account for diversity, contradiction and resistance? Theorists such as McKinnon assume that women are a homogeneous group; that we are all recipients of the male gaze and that we are passive in this process. In this sense, any sexually charged representation of women can be read as degrading, since it is seen to be produced by men for men. The role of women in this process is only ever to be able to look through the eyes of the male. We therefore become disempowered bodies which carry the fantasies of masculinity.

From this I wonder how political change can occur. Not only do these accounts lead to what Stacey[11] defines as the three options of masculinization, masochism or marginality; they also confine women to the passive reproduction of male power every time they breathe any sign of sexuality. If feminism is to speak to women, it at least needs to address their different sexualities and desires, and to recognize that sexuality is often one of the only resources that women can draw upon to overcome powerlessness. We can only exist within the discursive spaces and structures to which we have access. We are located and circumscribed by gender, race and class. However, if we use our female cultural capital of sexuality in ways that do not conform to the masculine defined norm we can challenge the legitimacy of masculinity (see Skeggs, 1991). Madonna, who specifically deals with the most explicit of pornographic images, argues that she is trying to challenge those who want to define her as a passive sex object. She says:

> A woman who is overtly sexual is considered a venomous bitch or someone to be feared. So what I like to do is take the traditional overtly sex-like bimbo image and turn it round to say I can dress this way, or behave this way but I'm in charge. I call the shots and I know what I'm doing. (BBC TV, *Omnibus*, December 1990)

Like many feminists such as Angela Carter and Carol Vance,[12] Madonna sees sexuality as much more than male domination. She begins with the currency of women's lives. Whilst sexuality, admittedly, is an area for control and violence against women, it can be about more than this. It is an area where women have been both dominated and can sometimes dominate. It's an area where women can take responsibility and lose it. They can also have fun and pleasure. Madonna argues that she focuses on sexuality because it is so central and so ubiquitous.

Prior Knowledge

The way people respond to Madonna is likely to be dependent on their economic and cultural location and their investments, hopes and despair. For instance, one group of fifteen-year-old, working-class girls, recently interviewed in York, felt they could not express approval of Madonna or they would not be seen to be respectable. They were frightened of being tarred with the brush of explicit sexuality. Others, more middle-class and hence already coded as more respectable, were less worried about the policing of their sexuality and more openly appreciative (Rowley).[13]

Responses are also dependent on intertextual references, as we have many sources of information on Madonna other than her records and videos. We know, for instance, that Madonna has not been manipulated in the way many other female artists have and that she has complete control over her own career. We also know that she has a great deal of financial power. The naming of her companies as Slutco Inc., Siren Films, BoyToy Inc. and WEBO Girl Publishing suggests an impudence that stretches to financial matters.

We also know that Madonna is very knowledgeable about art, photography, music and technology. The whole of the book *Sex* can be read as a reworking of different artistic forms. The first pages of lesbian sado-masochistic scenes are remarkably similar to Della Grace's *Love Bites*. The knowledge of Robert Mapplethorpe's black male photography helps us to understand other photographs in the book. However, we must be careful not to allow the pretensions of art to enable us to distance ourselves from the performative aspects of sexuality imaged in the book.

Prior knowledge of New York's club scene from which Madonna emerged can also help us understand the tactics which she deploys to deal with reactionary criticism. On the first night of the *Blond Ambition* tour some people complained about Madonna's swearing. Madonna reacted on the second night by completely over-the-top swearing. Outrage is the strategy she draws from the New York lesbian and gay scene which refuses to have its sexuality silenced.

Anyone with any prior knowledge of Madonna's own life who listens to the 'Hanky Panky' lyrics, which demand that someone spank her, have no doubt that she is in complete control. When she threatens to get cranky if she doesn't get her spanky we know she is being irreverent. We have previously heard the pain, anguish and despair on 'Till Death Us Do Part':

> The bruises, they will fade away
> You hit so hard with the things you say
> I will not stay to watch your hate as it grows
> You're not in love with someone else
> You don't even love yourself
> Still I wish you'd ask me not to go.
> She's had enough, she says the end
> But she'll come back, she knows it then
> A chance to start it all again
> Till death do us part

From this we learn that Madonna takes the issue of domestic violence and emotional attachment very seriously. We understand from the lyrics that she also works through contradictions. She openly articulates the complications and confusion experienced in violent relationships. She points to the cultural and economic investments that women may be locked into; including love, pain, romance and despair. In her personal life she divorced her husband, enabling her to escape from his violence: clearly, she had the resources to make such a move. In the book *Sex* all the constructions of sado-masochism were directed and selected by Madonna. Just in case we forget she keeps telling us, in the text, that these are fantasies. To make certain that we don't take them seriously the by now familiar technique of laughing to signify parodic distance is used. Irony is a constant stance in both the music and the videos. But Madonna is also serious.

Tracks such as 'Oh Father' and 'Keep it Together' work through difficult and contradictory emotions. These emotions are likely to be widely shared with many women. She tells of survival: 'You can't hurt me now', 'I made it through the wilderness', and 'Bye Bye Baby: this is the first time and the last time you'll ever see me cry'. McClary[14] maintains that the musical forms used by Madonna represent an aural survival against threat. Madonna expresses vulnerabilities and celebrates strengths. She articulates fear and fascination. She deals with the affective and the emotional by inserting desire and power into them. She makes the body an explicit site for the transmission of visual and aural affectivity, a feature often dismissed or ignored by male musicians in an attempt to make their music appear only cerebral. This again, is a specific centring of female experience.

Women Only

Madonna speaks to women's experiences. She directly addresses women, as in the videos and lyrics of 'Borderline', 'Papa don't Preach' and 'Express Yourself'. Prior knowledge of Madonna also reveals that whilst she has power and control, she also likes 'having a laugh'. The visual narrative is often disrupted when she looks straight at the camera and through self-conscious laughing compels us to laugh at the construction of the video images, as in 'Justify my Love', 'Cherish' and 'Hanky Panky'. 'Vogue' and 'Erotica' address the performative aspects of sexuality identified by Judith Butler.[15] Madonna addresses female audiences as if she were just one of the girls having a laugh. This is epitomized on the *Blond Ambition* Tour (1990) where, as one of the girls, she shouts out challenges to men's predatory behaviour, combining these with safe sex messages.

Madonna embodies the spirit of the girls' Friday night-out. Here the concerns are to have a laugh, to be fashionable and look good for your mates, possibly to have this confirmed by male desire, often to ridicule posing and pretentious men, and to have a good dance. More generally Friday night functions to make women feel good about themselves. Dance is an essential ingredient in the Madonna persona. It is dance for fun, for self-indulgence. It is a display of power, energy and vitality. Paradoxically it involves choreographed control over the body whilst displaying emotional abandonment, loss of oneself through music, and being out of reach of controlling forces. As Madonna's lyrics stated in 1984: 'Where's the party? I want to free my soul. Where's the party? I want to lose control'.

Whilst 'having a laugh' is a well-researched and well-documented means of coping with powerlessness, Madonna is actually able to have a different sort of laugh. She is not so constrained by the gender boundaries that control most of her audience. She is able to reappropriate the mechanisms that are used to control women: violence being the most coercive. She is able to use her power as a star to articulate the sexualities and fantasies that other women would be condemned for. Madonna is not content to just reproduce what we already have, she is concerned to challenge.

This speaking to women, the articulation of different possibilities of female sexuality: lesbianism, autonomous, fantastical, performative, is possibly why she has been so grossly misunderstood by male music critics. She is not speaking to them. Linda Williams[16] notes how pornography represents the male quest to understand the 'truth' of female sexuality, what she calls 'figuring the visual

The male gaze. But who has control? The eyes are soft, unfocused, submissive. Only Madonna confronts the camera eye directly. 'Power is a great aphrodisiac, and I'm a very powerful person'.

The Blonde Ambition tour.

"knowledge" of women's pleasure'. It is another way in which women are made the object of male knowledge. Hence pornography dwells on the biology and technology of sex. It is not able to deal with a female sexuality constructed by women, for it would be outside of the boundaries of this knowledge. Thus when Madonna takes the tools of pornography and uses them to suggest a pleasure in herself and other women that is unavailable to men, it is quite likely that she will become incomprehensible to those for whom porn was designed.

Madonna uses her sexuality to expose its working and she uses the currency of pornography to challenge the idea of women as passive objects. The video 'Open Your Heart' is the most obvious indictment of the objectification of women by men, and the destruction of innocence, fun and pleasure as a result. In the video the gaze is (yet again) reversed, it is shown from the eyes of the woman who performs pornographic acts for the men who pay to peep through a small screen. As their money runs out and the screen slowly closes they are shown contorting to try and see through the last minute slit. They look pathetic, silly and desperate. We are given a range of different types of men (even 'academics' making notes) so they cannot be written off as stereotypical 'perverts'. We can pity them, laugh at them. As individuals their power is destroyed. It is the institutionalization of their power in the pornography industry that is located as the problem in the video.

When Madonna simulates masturbation on stage, to the horror of her male dancers, she is making a massive global audience aware of her transgression. She speaks to an autonomous female sexuality which is not dependent on the services of men. By advocating *Pussy Power*, (again appropriated from lesbian relations of sexuality) the insatiability and power of the clitoris, signifying female sexuality, is cherished and put onto a public and popular agenda. And visibility and confirmation is given to lesbian sexuality.

Madonna, both on stage and in her own life, expresses desire for and celebrates intimacy with other women. Her friendship with Sandra Bernhard and the much publicized tongue kissing with the star of the film *Nikita*, Naomi Campbell and Isabella Rossellini are part of a refusal to be contained within heterosexuality. *The Sun* attempted to trivialize and dismiss such behaviour. In the video 'Justify my Love' the man looks on with confusion whilst Madonna displays her pleasure in another woman. This video in particular can be construed as a male pornographic fantasy, but is the expression of female sexuality ever free from the possibility of fetishization? The pages of the *Sunday Sport* made lesbianism one of the most marketable of male fantasies and yet nobody would suggest that lesbians should stop being so just because they can be appropriated.

Madonna speaks to women by using their cultural currency. On the *Like a Virgin* (1984) tour she addressed the patriarchal controls on young women by actually having her own father pull her off the stage when she was clearly enjoying herself. In the more recent videos 'Justify my Love' and 'Erotica' she addresses those who are more confident and assured of their sexual desires. She now speaks to women who feel confident and powerful with their sexuality.

Using Men

Madonna reverses the gaze by subjecting men to the scrutiny of her gaze. Looking at men is treated as something to be blatant and positive about rather than surreptitious. The black and Hispanic men she uses in her videos and concerts signify sexually powerful masculinities. This can be seen as racist if one does not have prior knowledge of her commitment to anti-racism.

Madonna also de-stabilizes representations of male power through humorous humiliation. Not since Mae West have we seen such playful denigration. Male humiliation is often a source of pleasure for those who are rendered powerless in other spheres of life. In the best ironic tradition, Madonna enables us (women) to laugh at and momentarily undermine those who control us. The mermen in the 'Cherish' video, and particularly on the *Blond Ambition* (1990) tour force us to laugh at their absurdity. The 'Did You Do It?' track on *Erotica* is a hilarious undermining of the macho celebrations of rap misogyny. One rapper brags about having sex with a woman whilst his mates ask 'did you do it?'. 'I did it' is his continual response. The music of 'Waiting' plays in the background, towards the end becoming louder so all we hear is Madonna singing 'still waiting' whilst the rapper claims in a more desperate voice to his mates that he did it.

The use of men is constantly changing. In some videos these men are set up as powerful, only to be ultimately under her control. In others she de-sexualizes them, as in the use of hermaphrodite costumes on the *Blond Ambition Tour* (1990). In others, such as the 'Burning Up' video, they become irrelevant. She plays with and de-stabilizes the fixing and categorization of male sexuality in much the same way as she does with female sexuality.

Madonna also expresses her gratitude to men for making her feel good, as in 'Like a Virgin' – 'You make me feel shiny and new' – and 'Cherish' – 'You got the power to make me feel good'. In a recent interview with Carrie Fisher[17] Madonna articulates the little respect she has for heterosexual men, despairing over the fact that she cannot meet a man who knows more than she does. There is no uni-dimensionality to Madonna's responses. She operates on a continuum of expression. She condemns and appreciates. She is serious and she laughs. Just like most women really.

Sexual Expression

Rarely are women free to express themselves sexually; it has even been argued that women do not have a discourse in which to speak desire. Yet Madonna articulates female desire as a right – 'I want' is a persistent theme in her work.

She says how she wants it (as in 'Justify my Love' and 'Erotica') and yet is aware of how desire constrains, as in 'Borderline': 'Something in the way you love me won't let me be'. Nevertheless, desire is usually on her terms, with an in-built awareness that this will vacillate between the rational message of 'He needs to start with your head. Satin sheets are very romantic. What happens when you're not in bed' and the 'irrationality' of her own passion and desire; she's often burning up. In 'Express Yourself' she argues that the chain around her neck is a metaphor for sexual desire:

> It's ironic and controversial, to change everything, to ask what if it was like this and that. No matter how in control you think you are of sexuality and relationships there is always a certain amount of compromise, always a certain amount of beholden if in love. You're not in control even if you think so. But it's something that you choose to do. Nobody put the chain around my neck. I was chained to my desire.
> (BBC TV, *Omnibus*, December 1990)

The continual use of sado-masochistic imagery may signify the vacillation between control and loss of oneself. However, you have to have control before you can lose it. Reynolds[18] notes how loss, being 'blissed out', is a recurring theme of white male music. To generalize, rap evokes the opposite; it is about taking control. Madonna moves between the two.

Anyone who wants to confine analysis of Madonna to the tart-victim category should ask themselves if they could ever imagine her not being in control. Her sexual armour-plated costumes are the ultimate product of the logic of punk bricolage that she began with: they say 'I am a sexual being, on my terms, I am not here for your benefit but for mine'. Williamson[19] argues that Madonna's wearing of underwear on the outside of her costumes is a metaphor for wearing desire on one's sleeve.

Masquerade

Madonna (like Bowie and Prince) has always played with multiple subjectivities that vacillate between gender categories. Whilst her continual change of image is an effective marketing strategy, it also demonstrates, as Heath (1986)[20] and Walkerdine (1989)[21] argue, that femininity is a masquerade and performance. Madonna makes public and exalts the masquerade and performance e.g. the Dita personality for the expression of sexual fantasies in *Sex* (taken from the 1930s actress Dita Parlo). She operates on a continuum of gender, moving around the power associated with certain categories. She takes delight in the female competence of reconstruction. On the record sleeve to 'Justify my Love' she combines gay male S&M imagery, with Monroe features and James Dean stance as she stares defiantly at the camera. *Sex* is an ironic homage to many of the images of femininity that women have been constrained by. 'Vogue' and 'Erotica' are based solely on playful performances, appropriated from the black and white gay male New York cultures.

Judith Butler[22] believes that such playing can only lead to the eventual destruction of compulsory heterosexuality and its accompanying power relations:

> Hence there is a subversive laughter in the pastiche-effect of parodic practices in which the original, the authentic and the real are themselves constituted as effects. The loss of gender norms would have the effect of proliferating gender configuration, destabilizing substantive identity, and depriving the naturalizing narratives of compulsory heterosexuality. (p.146)

Popular culture, especially music, is a prime site for challenges. Bricolage, appropriation and pastiche enable the popular to remain popular. They were in operation long before post-modern theorists claimed them as their own. By playing popular culture so well Madonna is able to use its spaces to make challenges. They may not be perfect, sometimes even problematic, but if they contribute to a shifting of the discursive boundaries that control the expression of women's sexuality and a breakdown of the institutional barriers constructed out of women's silence, they are doing more than mere acquiescence. Madonna attempts to take on board the seriousness of sexual power and objectification whilst retaining a sense of humour. It is a difficult position. But to laugh rather than to despair may be a more effective preparation for the continual challenges necessary in the hegemonic battle over who is able to define and speak sexuality.

If young women do not have to monitor their bodies and their attitudes on a daily basis for *fear* of being seen to be sexual, something has been achieved. We can only fight with the cultural resources to which we have access. For some it is education, for others it is sexuality, for others it is both. Hegemonic masculinity will always try to define and confine female sexuality. The important thing is to resist male meanings. Madonna is the queen of the undermining of masculinity; it is a tradition which has a long history in both camp and working class women's cultures. To give it public credibility is no bad thing.

To conclude, power and control in sexuality and pleasure in my body are things I'd like to aspire to. It has greater personal/political value than believing that I'm always going to be a victim of male domination. Madonna uses the power she has at her disposal to challenge the certainties of sexual identity and gender constraint. The greater the range of sites in which male domination is challenged the better as far as I'm concerned. Wanting to have a good time, having fun and being sexual without being condemned for it, whilst still being politically challenging speaks to me about my life. I don't want to be the surveillant of my own sexuality – I want to appreciate it. I share the frustrations Madonna articulates on 'Why's it so hard' on *Erotica*:

> What do I have to do to be accepted
> What do I have to say

What do I have to do to be respected
What do I have to play
What do I have to look like to feel I'm equal
Where do I have to go
What club to I have to join to feel I'm worthy
Who do I have to know
Chorus:
I'm telling you, brothers, sisters
Why can't we learn to challenge the system
Without living in pain

I'm really pleased that Madonna enables women to laugh at the male fantasies that can often contain the expression of female sexuality. Like Prince, she operates at the boundaries of normalization – she keeps issues of sexual power on the agenda and she gives women a space to laugh publicly at the pretence and precariousness of masculine constructions of sexuality. She also provides an example of how women can be strong and in control, whilst also having to deal with vulnerability and oppression. She, along with other women musicians, such as BWP, Roxanne Shante, Adeva and She Rockers have enabled a discursive realignment: words such as insolent, defiant, impudent, strong, autonomous, independent and powerful are now more easily aligned with sexually-active young women. Madonna suggests to her audience that it is possible to overcome the daily humiliations of sexism with the power of enjoyment. My own ethnographic work[23] demonstrates that many young women have feminist attitudes which they, unlike Madonna have to negotiate against other cultural and economic investments. Madonna offers aspirations and fantasies that can be used to increase self-esteem, as the following comments by two fifteen-year olds, taken from a research project in the North of England, indicate:

> It's like after you've watched her on telly or something, you walk, no you flaunt out of the room, thinking, well if she can, why can't I . . . mind you my brother then asks why I'm walking so stupid and I soon come back to earth.

> We always put her on before we go out on a Friday night. It makes you feel good. It makes us feel stroppy, like we could take on anything. Yea, it makes you feel, like, good in yourself.

Such comments contain the idealized fantasy of control against the grim and humiliating everyday. They represent momentary relief against powerlessness. They don't resign women to fatalistic despair, but offer the possibility of something better. At the affective level Madonna can make young women feel good about themselves. It's a start and nobody else seems to be doing it on such a global scale.

6 'I ALWAYS GET MY MAN': Madonna and Dick Tracy

Richard Reynolds

> ... seduction represents mastery over the symbolic universe, while power represents only mastery of the real universe.
> Jean Baudrillard[1]

> 'Tess, there's about as much chance of me getting behind a desk as there is of me getting a new girlfriend.'
> From the film *Dick Tracy*[2]

When Oklahoma-born Chester Gould created Dick Tracy for the newspaper strips in 1931, the character was known as Plainclothes-man Tracy. Joseph Medell Patterson of the Chicago Tribune Syndi-cate preferred the name Dick. The change was a fortunate one: Dick Tracy of the Gould comics is undoubtedly an archetypal 'Dick', in both the law-enforcement and phallic senses of the word.

Gould's Tracy inhabits an America in which good and evil are absolutely distinct, with none of the moral shades and ambiguities that typify the more sophisticated adventure strips of the thirties and forties. Tracy is an official agent of the law, not a private eye like contemporaries Slam Bradley or Rip Kirby.[3] Tracy is faithfully and chastely involved with girlfriend Tess Trueheart, though his fidelity is not subjected to severe testing. Tracy is upright, loyal, incorrupt-ible: an able and resourceful upholder of the law. He employs the latest and even futuristic technology (lie detectors, wristwatch radios) and offers in the 'Crimestopper's Handbook' detection tips to trap real-life crooks. By way of contrast, the villains of the Dick Tracy comics present a gallery of the malformed in body and mind: the incomprehensible Mumbles, the wrinkly Pruneface, the level-headed Flattop, the reclusive Mole, or the crazy eight-foot woman cab driver known as Acres O'Riley.[4]

Warren Beatty's 1990 movie *Dick Tracy* adopts the unrelentingly ironic stance which seems to be the norm for films based on comic book characters. Tracy's antics in pursuit of Big Boy, Pruneface, Mumbles and the rest are pitched at the level of a stylish satire, taking the form but not the mood of the comics as their spring-board. Madonna is cast as nightclub chanteuse Breathless Mahoney, Tracy's would-be seducer. On stage, she delivers several songs which play an important part in setting the tone of the movie and underscoring its themes: 'I Always Get My Man', 'More', 'Now I'm Following You'.[5] As the steamy seductress, she has four major scenes during which Dick's fidelity to Tess Trueheart (Glenne Headly) is put under increasingly severe pressure. These scenes are the most intriguing in the movie, and develop a screen persona for Madonna which can be seen as a logical extension of her music and video output. Moreover, as these scenes are not satires on the comic – Dick Tracy comics lack the seduction motif – they are played 'straight'.

The first of these scenes occurs after Breathless's lover Lips Manlis has been murdered by rival mobster Big Boy (played by Al Pacino). Breathless skilfully switches her allegiance to Big Boy, who is happy to claim her as part of his spoils. Tracy is convinced that Breathless has evidence that will help put Big Boy behind bars for the Manlis killing. Wearing his trademark tan-yellow hat and overcoat, he bursts into Breathless's changing room during a raid on Big Boy's club. Breathless asks if he's going to arrest her. 'If I was gonna arrest you, I'd have done it by now' answers Tracy. He explains his suspicions about the Manlis murder, then asks Breathless whose side she's on. 'Mine' replies Breathless. Dick tries to interrogate her, but is sidetracked at every juncture by Breathless's verbal seduction. 'No grief for Lips?' asks Dick. 'I'm wearing black underwear' replies Breathless.

The room is in near-darkness: Tracy's tan-yellow clothes are the only splash of colour apart from Breathless's platinum blonde hair and red lips. The hair, the lips, black dress (it might be a negligee) and sultry voice overdetermine Breathless as the seductress. The scene's narrative content is so manifest in the first lines of dialogue that attention is easily diverted away from its closure towards the overload of signs – visual, verbal, gestural.

Both sides of the dialogue involve a lot of questions. Tracy, as the detective and embodiment of masculine function and order, asks questions which seek specific information ('Whose side are you on?') or attempt to impose control ('Maybe you weren't on his side?'). Breathless's questions are different, opening up the conversation and diverting it from the logic of interrogation ('Aren't you gonna arrest me?'). To seduce (se ducere), is to lead away, and Breathless effortlessly seduces Tracy from his interrogation by subversion of the detective's own vocabulary ('Sit down. Aren't you gonna arrest me?') or the processes of the law itself:

DICK

You know it's legal for me to take you down to the station and sweat it out of you under the lights?

BREATHLESS

I sweat a lot better in the dark . . .

The seduction is successful. Dick enters the room in control of the situation: the cop in the middle of making an arrest. He leaves confused, no longer the master of his fate ('Big Boy's in jail. You're the one who can keep him there. Give me a call.')

Tracy's second encounter with Breathless occurs when she pays a call on him at the police station. This time they are on Tracy's territory, an austere and heavily masculine office. Tracy sits at his desk. Breathless approaches down a long corridor dressed in a low-cut evening gown with towering padded shoulders. In Marilyn Monroe's staccato diction, she asks Tracy what a girl has to do to get arrested. 'Wearing that dress is a step in the right direction' Dick replies.

The scene develops along the lines of their previous encounter, Dick deflecting advances via the alibi of professionalism; 'I'm on duty'. Breathless drapes herself across Dick's desk, but his resistance is stalwart as he stares Breathless straight in the eye, asking if she's ready to testify. Breathless kisses him, but he doesn't respond.

BREATHLESS

> You're right, Tracy. Why should you get mixed
> up with me? I'm a cheap floozy to you. I'll be
> lucky if I get through this week alive . . .

Once again, Breathless undermines Dick's rhetorical strategy, diverting the process of detection into the discourse of seduction. Tracy can't use Breathless as a witness without deepening his involvement with her as a seductress – without becoming even more 'mixed up' with her.

The third meeting provokes a crisis. Breathless unexpectedly visits Tracy's apartment. Again, they play the game of question versus question. Dick asks Breathless twice what she's doing in his home. Breathless removes her coat, revealing her strapless black evening gown. 'Aren't you gonna frisk me?' she asks huskily.

The conversation turns to her possible testimony against Big Boy, now free and running the city's rackets again. Tracy promises that if Breathless testifies he will protect her '24 hours a day'. Breathless asks if he always puts so much of himself into his job. Tracy says she won't know until she testifies. Has Tracy turned at least in part from seduced to seducer? His reticence seems to have made him still more desirable to Breathless. She calls him a good man and says she wants to 'do the right thing'. They kiss, but are interrupted by the arrival of Tess and Tracy's boy assistant. Breathless leaves, but Tess has seen enough to be provoked into a crisis of jealousy.

The final Breathless/Dick scene completes their reversal of roles. Detective and witness meet at a deserted riverside wharf. Again, they play the game of questions while the dialogue implies a formal opposition between the processes of detection and seduction.

> BREATHLESS
>
> . . . You want me. Don't you?

> DICK
>
> You're right. I do want you. In court.
> Where you can tell the truth.

Breathless tells Dick he's lying: 'You want me the same way I want you.' Tracy repeats his offer of protection if Breathless agrees to testify. But Breathless tells him she can't trust a man who won't reveal his feelings:

> DICK
>
> Wait a minute! What do you want me
> to admit? That I think about you?
> OK. I admit it. Testify!

> BREATHLESS
>
> You want my testimony? Tell me
> you want me. If you do that I'll do
> anything you say. How bad do you want
> Big Boy? It's up to you. Tell me you
> want me. Tell me you want it all. But
> tell me now.

But Dick's loyalty to Tess is the bottom line. 'You trust her?' asks Breathless, her final question. 'I love her' is his reply. The die is cast. Breathless begins to plot in secret (and in a masculine disguise) to get Tracy out of the way – a task at which Big Boy's mobsters have been notably unsuccessful. At the film's denouement, Breathless's disguise is penetrated by Tracy as she lies dying, leaving him free of further temptation and still faithful to Tess Trueheart.

On the face of it, Breathless's confident boast that 'I always get my man' is an empty one, even if Madonna herself was involved with Warren Beatty during the making of the movie. Is the film simply a cosy fable of the virtuous woman's triumph over the seductress? This is certainly the way in which the plot unfolds, but to read the movie as a whole in this light is to ignore the subtext of the Madonna/Warren Beatty scenes and the energies set up by the audience's intertextual expectations from Madonna's work as a whole.[6] And it would also mean ignoring the presence of Madonna's personal commentary on the Dick Tracy movie: the *I'm Breathless* album of 'Music from and inspired by the movie Dick Tracy'.

If Dick wins the movie, Madonna certainly comes out on top in the album. Dick Tracy is the protagonist of the movie, successfully 'tracing' what lies hidden and ultimately controlling the unfolding narrative. The album is, not surprisingly, centred around Madonna's persona and performance. In several of the songs she presents Dick Tracy as the passive object of Breathless's desire. Although the musical style varies from forties pastiche to contemporary dance numbers such as 'Vogue', the tendency of the lyrics and delivery at all times encourage the listener to identify with Madonna herself. She dominates, for example, the vocal duet with Warren Beatty in 'Now I'm Following You', and in 'He's a Man' effectively reduces the detective-as-sex-symbol to an easily manipulated fetish figure.

'Vogue' and the swing-beat 'Hanky Panky' have little or no narrative connection to the movie, yet both offer a powerful thematic counterpoint to the seduction motif. 'Hanky Panky' achieved a certain notoriety in 1990 for its mild S&M connotations – now thoroughly upstaged by Madonna's book *Sex*. 'Hanky Panky' is the song of a woman happy to demand exactly what she wants:

> Treat me like I'm a bad girl
> Even when I'm being good to you . . .
> Tie my hands behind my back
> And ooh I'm in ecstasy

The ironic counterpoint of the album may also lead to a reinterpretation of the movie. Is it loyalty to Tess Trueheart which stops Dick Tracy sleeping with Breathless Mahoney? Another reading is possible, one in which Breathless does 'get her man'. The dialogue and acting have set up an effective opposition between detection and seduction, but Breathless's final offer is one of truth in return for sex – a complete subversion of Tracy's detective persona and his machismo. Tracy is manoeuvred into a position where his detection comes to depend on his sexuality. Faced with the unacceptable option of putting his sexuality at the service of his job, he chooses the only way out: the protection of his loyalty to Tess. It is a choice which preserves his detective's power over events, yet the significance of his actions and even his ideology have been indelibly redefined by his contact with Breathless. Conversely, Breathless's control throughout of the movie's symbolic discourse is a reflection of Madonna's control of and seduction of her audience as a whole.

'Aren't you gonna frisk me?' Breathless Mahoney pays a call on Dick Tracy. It's Tess Trueheart's photograph she has in her hands.

7 Telling Tales: Madonna, *Sex* and the British Press

C. Kay Weaver

For some weeks prior to the publication *Sex*[1] the British media indulged in an obsessive affair with Madonna. Declaring 14 October 1992 'Madonna Day', BBC Radio One broadcast an interview with the star and devoted considerable air time to her records. The previous night Madonna appeared in a highly publicized television interview with Channel Four's chat show host Jonathan Ross. Journalists wired reports from New York on the launch party for *Sex*. Those bastions of British culture, the novelist Martin Amis and newspaper editor Andrew Neil, crossed the Atlantic to meet and assess the star in person for their own publications. His mission a failure, Amis returned leaving *The Observer* with exclusive pictures from *Sex* but no interview. Neil got the interview but the *Sunday Times* lacked the accompanying pictures. Other writers gave commentaries on the whole bonanza of reporting and, when it was finally released, then offered their opinions of *Sex* itself.

Radio and television were constrained in how much attention they could devote to Madonna and *Sex*. Broadcast media have schedules to maintain and air time is limited. Newspapers, in contrast, have more available space enabling journalists to report and analyse issues in greater detail and depth. Unconstrained by the demands of objectivity and balance, print journalists also have more freedom in what they can write. How then did the British press report Madonna in relation to the publication of *Sex*?

Reporting Madonna

The British mainstream national press consists of both popular and quality newspapers. Tabloid in format, popular newspapers depend on sales for revenue. Broadsheet quality newspapers gain their revenue by selling advertising space. The revenue source of newspapers directly affects news reporting. Popular papers, having to maximize sales for profit appeal to readers through 'lowest common denominator' journalism. This consists of stories 'with a sensational theme, preferably involving sexual scandal or crime, popular "celebrities" or public figures'.[2] Such papers are generally purchased by readers of the economically and educationally poorer social classes. The quality press, taking revenue from advertisers, seek readers with disposable incomes with which to purchase advertised products. Their reporting style appeals to a middle-class readership of a higher educational standard. Thus, the structure of the press is reflective of the class and educational divisions in British society.[3]

Reflective of their marketing strategy, the tabloids featured the greater number of stories about Madonna and *Sex*. Although quality newspapers devoted fewer stories to this subject, reports were greater in length and detail than those of the tabloids. Quality papers often covered with one story the angles which a tabloid paper might take several articles and even several days to report. Characteristically, the tabloids used attention-grabbing headlines and prominent pictures in their reporting. The qualities generally adopted a more subtle, up-market approach giving less prominence to pictures and headlines.

The written style of the reports also differed across the newspaper types. Tabloid journalists wrote with emotional charge, often declaring feelings of outrage, shock or alternatively utter boredom toward Madonna. Journalists for the qualities usually adopted a more detached and objective style of reporting. Despite the differences in the number of stories and their visual and written style, there were, however, many thematic commonalities across the newspapers in what was said about Madonna and *Sex*. These reveal an overwhelmingly conservative and often blatantly sexist and homophobic press reaction to *Sex*. Moreover, the press self-righteously criticized Madonna for doing exactly what it seeks to do itself – make money.

The Queen of hype

A relationship of mutual dependence operates between stars and the press. Stars seek publicity to sell themselves and their products. As stated, stories about stars sell papers – especially tabloids. Publishing a book of explicit photographs of her sexual fantasies, Madonna gave the press a highly saleable story. However, evident in many reports was a pretence of resentment toward Madonna for gaining such free publicity. This was partly due to the explicit nature of Madonna's book, but also because Madonna was 'calling the shots' in her dealings with the media. Unusually in the case of a book publication, Madonna, as author of *Sex*, commanded absolute control over its pre-publication publicity. No review copies of *Sex* were released and journalists were permitted to view the book only under strict monitoring and on signing a contract of confidentiality. Gaining interviews with Madonna was even more precarious, with several agreements to speak to journalists being later withdrawn. Journalists used to being a position of power over publicity-seeking authors and celebrities were, on this occasion, in danger of appearing like rats running after a pied-piping Madonna. The response from the press was to condemn Madonna as a conjurer of hype.

Numerous newspaper articles portrayed Madonna as a manipulative self-publicist. The *Daily Mirror* asked 'Is Madonna . . . a sexual crusader, an icon for the young or a phoney interested in her own hype?'[4] The *Guardian*'s report, headlined 'Unclad icon screened by wall of hype', described Madonna as orchestrating all her media dealings for maximum publicity effect.[5] The *Daily Mail*, reporting on the New York launch of *Sex*, declared 'Madonna's pathetic quest to shock (and hype her new book) continues'.[6] Other articles described Madonna as 'the high priestess of hype, the mistress of manipulation',[7] 'The Queen of hype',[8] 'a Picasso of self-promotion, an Eisenstein of media hype'.[9] Madonna was, then, held in contempt (by both the tabloid and quality press) for exploiting the fact that stories about stars are the bread and butter of many a newspaper journalist.

Some reports were more objective about Madonna's relationship with the media. The *Independent* discussed Madonna in the context of an entertainment industry concerned with not only creating publicity and profits for its stars but also for itself.[10] In the *Guardian*, Suzanne Moore went further and explained why the press were so sensitive about Madonna's dealings with the media:

> What upsets us most though is not the nakedness of her body but the nakedness of her ambition. For all her antics, all she ever exposes are the mechanics of stardom in the late twentieth century.[11]

As indicated by Moore, Madonna's ability to draw publicity is largely due to her market manipulation: she promises to reveal the truth about herself in her latest product but never really does.[12] However, the press are prepared to play along with this because as long as Madonna is able to manipulate her markets she remains 'news'. Some attempted to deny this. Martin Amis in the *Observer* declared '*Sex* is no more than the desperate confection of an ageing scandal-addict who, with this book, merely confirms that she is exhausting her capacity to shock.'[13] The *Daily Mail* announced that 'after a while you become immune' to Madonna's attempts to shock.[14] Nevertheless, there is no denying that Madonna's antics were shocking enough to warrant considerable newspaper coverage.

'Don't you realize that this is a publicity stunt?' [*Sex*] Madonna and Tony Ward in the 'Justify My Love' video.

Sex as pornography

What does and what does not constitute pornography is a complicated issue. Equally contentious is whether pornography is socially acceptable. There are different forms of pornography from soft core to hard core and, as Linda Williams notes, 'one person's pornography is another person's erotica'.[15] Madonna would have been aware that *Sex* would be classed as pornographic and that she would be highly criticized for its production. However, when the book was thus criticized little explanation was given as to why it did constitute pornography and not erotica. Also apparent here is the hypocrisy of the tabloid press. These papers, and especially the *Sun*, are notorious for featuring women in soft porn poses yet they criticize Madonna for being pornographic. Another issue was the *Observer*'s exclusive publication of a number of pictures from *Sex*. As the *Sun* was quick to point out[16] this was equally hypocritical, given the *Observer* editor's condemnation of tabloids for publishing soft porn.

Although Madonna claimed that *Sex* was not pornographic the *Daily Express* disagreed. In a front page story headlined 'Madonna: My book isn't porn' the paper made its own view known by stating: '*Sex*, the outrageous new book in which Madonna *appears in pornographic poses,* is innocent and artistic the singer claimed last night.'[17] Ten days later the *Express* announced that 'Madonna's *pornographic book, Sex,* was branded tacky, tawdry and an insult to women last night – but they still flocked to buy it.'[18] Other tabloids reported reactions from members of the public. The *Sun* quoted women as stating of *Sex* that 'If this was made into a film it would be nothing but porn', 'it is hardcore porn promoting nothing that could be truly pleasurable' and '*Sex* has set women's causes back by years'. One woman referred to the difficulty of defining pornography in remarking 'I suppose you would describe some of the photos as pornographic but the boundaries are forever changing.'[19] The *Daily Star* painted quite a different picture of women's reaction to *Sex*. Headlined 'Sex with Madonna will put a smile on your face,' the report stated that 'broad-minded Brits laughed off the contents and insisted "Sex with Madonna has really made us smile".'[20] The most supportive write up came from *Today*. The paper claimed that *Sex* represented a 'kind of revenge for women'. It was argued that *Sex* at last demonstrated to men what it was like to be portrayed in degrading images.[21]

The quality press were less sympathetic to *Sex* than *Today*. The *Observer* and the *Guardian* accused Madonna of being naive about pornography. Both papers quoted Madonna's statement in *Sex* that 'Generally I don't think pornography degrades women. The women doing it want to do it.'[22] Newspaper readers were rightly cautioned from glibly accepting such a view and reminded that the vast majority of women working in the pornography industries do so because there are no other options available to them. They were reminded that for many women pornography is either a desperate attempt to earn a living or an industry into which they are forced by those more powerful than themselves.

The *Observer* and the *Guardian*'s objections to Madonna's conceptions of pornography reflect feminist social-concern reactions. The *Sunday Telegraph*'s criticisms were, however, of quite a different order. In an article essentially condoning pornography, representatives of the porn industry were invited to remark on Madonna's suitability as a porn model.[23] From the more liberal *Observer* and *Guardian* the argument was that Madonna should be less naive about the nature of the pornography industry and the messages which she communicates about it. From the conservative *Sunday Telegraph* the argument was that Madonna lacked the qualifications needed to operate in that industry.

Morality in danger?

The question whether *Sex* was pornographic constituted part of a moral backlash against Madonna. On a number of occasions in the press Madonna was portrayed as threatening the moral well being of society.

Reflecting the ideology of the New Right[24] was the declaration that Madonna was posing a threat to family values. Gary Bushell, television critic for the *Sun*, argued that 'Madonna is saying: Sex is nasty, grubby, violent, promiscuous. Sex is anything goes. Except anything to do with love, affection, fidelity or family values.'[25] The *Daily Express*, describing Madonna as 'one of the most influential pop stars in the world', said 'But this fact has not stopped her from descending into a raunchy sleazy pit with a book that is so obviously contemptuous of the new mood of America which is embracing decent, family values.'[26] Such comments prevailed within many reports. Madonna was accused of promoting promiscuity in the face of AIDS and of exploiting liberal censorship laws, prompting the *Daily Telegraph* to conclude: 'In a world where nothing is taboo the amoral slut is queen.'[27]

Moral criticism is not something exclusively reserved for Madonna. It features in much newspaper reporting and especially tabloid reporting of 'personalities'. Connell argues that stories about the (usually private) antics of personalities are not only 'revealing tales, but also tales which set out to teach moral lessons by exposing unworthy and unbecoming actions. Moreover, though perhaps less surprisingly, the moral lessons they teach are relatively simple and conservative ones.'[28] The moral lessons given in reaction to Madonna and *Sex* were nowhere more explicitly given than in the *Sunday Times* which stated that:

> Madonna was clever enough to capture the currency of the age. The 1980s were built on greed, materialism, unemotional sex and a set of dumb bells. Now Madonna is old fashioned. The spirit of the 1990s is Demi Moore. Moore's got her man, Bruce Willis. She has a blossoming career and a body to match, which she claims giving birth to two children has drastically improved. She has maintained elegance and vulnerability, despite posing pregnant and naked for the cover of *Vanity Fair*, and she has sacrificed nothing for fame.[29]

The moral of this tale? If women want to 'get their man', have children, be perceived as elegant, vulnerable and feminine, thereby gaining respect, they should neither do as Madonna does nor try to emulate her.

Why does she do it?

While condemning Madonna for being a self-publicist and threat to morality, journalists simultaneously strove to provide psychological explanations for her behaviour. The *Sun* invited a psychotherapist and a psychologist to give their 'expert verdict' on *Sex*. The verdict was that Madonna's childhood, her Catholic upbringing, being raped when she was 20 years old and the death of her mother had left her extremely disturbed. Thus, the images in *Sex* became examples of how Madonna was (inadequately) dealing with her traumas and were reflective of, as the headline stated 'A tortured mind'.[30] The *Sun*'s Agony Aunt, Deirdre Sanders, gave a similar diagnosis explaining: 'Madonna is terrified of trusting. Hurt badly as a child, she must feel she is keeping control. Loving, trusting in being loved, means letting go and that's impossible for her.'[31] Although the *Daily Mirror* also reported Madonna's inner traumas it was unwilling to accept these as justification for *Sex* remarking 'It sounds like an adolescent cry for help. . . . A touching excuse more than a valid reason for what she does.'[32]

Madonna has frequently stated that her childhood has had an impact on what she does and how she does it.[33] Therefore, the 'expert analysis' exemplified in the *Sun* is hardly revealing or original. Madonna has also, however, quite poignantly remarked that 'in America absolutely no one is allowed to be successful and happy at the same time. They always manage to come up with some sort of tragic tale about you.'[34] Madonna's observation is an acute one. Portraying the rich and famous as unhappy and unfulfilled, the media become accomplices to an ideology which persuades those without wealth that money is not the route to happiness. The portrayal of the wealthy and glamorous yet forever troubled characters in *Dallas* is a typical example of this.

A confused sexuality?

There are few stars who parade their bodies and sexuality before the world quite to the extent that Madonna has. Portraying herself in sadomasochistic poses, as bisexual and fantasizing about being naked in public, Madonna's sex life frequently became a focus of attention in newspaper reports. Many of these reports contain underlying homophobic attitudes and conceptions of what is beyond the boundaries of 'normal' sexual practice. Not solely attributable to individual journalists, these attitudes are symptomatic of the culture in which we live. Were this not the case there would be public outcry rather than silent acceptance of such stories.

The question as to whether Madonna had had a lesbian affair was frequently raised by journalists. Andrew Neil put this to her in his *Sunday Times* interview, though he did so somewhat indirectly: 'Take the number of lesbian pictures in your book. Yet you have always been very coy about whether you had a lesbian affair with Sandra Bernhard [an American comedienne].' Madonna replied that she did not see of what relevance it was whom she slept with. To Neil it clearly was relevant. He pursued the question: 'Lesbianism is still for some a taboo subject: wouldn't it have made sense, by terms of your own mission, for you to say "Yes I did sleep with Sandra, and I am proud of it?"' With this Neil got the reply he wanted – that there had been no affair. In deploying a pretence of being concerned about social attitudes toward lesbianism Neil had called Madonna's bluff. He cared little about lesbianism at all: he had, as he stated got 'an admission' and a journalistic exposé.[35]

Neil's approach to the issue of Madonna's sexuality mirrors Armitage *et al*'s findings on the treatment of homosexuals by the British press. They state that 'The homosexuality of some stars, as "revealed" by the press, [is] presented as undermining appropriate gender behaviour in order to preserve the myth of the heterosexual norm. Frequently stars are asked to deny the rumours.'[36] Indeed, several reports explicitly condemned Madonna for being sexually abnormal. The *Daily Telegraph* wrote of *Sex* featuring Madonna in 'gay sex' which was described as a 'human perversion'.[37] Martin Amis stated of Madonna that *Sex* 'shows how over evolved and tangential her own sexuality has become'.[38] Chrissey Iley in the *Sunday Times* stated that Madonna 'doesn't know what her sexuality is any more.'[39] These latter two stories portray Madonna's sexuality as malfunctioning or confused. In effect they reject bisexuality and homosexuality as being a matter of rational preference.

Madonna's denial of the affair with Sandra Bernhard was reported in both the *Sun* ('Star denies fling with gay Sandra') and *Today*.[40] It was reported that Madonna allowed people to believe in the affair to help the cause of homosexuals. These stories, whilst portraying Madonna as sympathetic to homosexuals, celebrate the fact that she is, in fact, heterosexual and, therefore, 'normal'.

Prior to Madonna's denial of the lesbian affair the *Daily Star* ran a story headlined 'She and Sandra give stud Beatty a sex night he will never forget'. Here Warren Beatty was cast as a macho 'super stud'. It is alleged that Madonna and Sandra Bernhard kissed in front of Beatty on Madonna's first date with him and that he 'didn't bat an eyelid'. Beatty is quoted as saying 'They were so hot for each other that I wondered if I was going to be surplus to requirements.' Madonna, we are told, was testing Beatty's reaction and his cool handling of the situation 'turned the girls onto him.'[41] It is a story which reproduces images found in hardcore pornographic films where 'the "lesbian" number [scene] is presented . . . as a warm-up or rehearsal for a "better", more satisfying, number that will follow.'[42] What is significant about the imagery evoked in the report is the 'deviancy' of Madonna and Bernhard in comparison to the 'super stud' quality of Beatty. This reflects a highly sexist view of female homosexuality: lesbianism is acceptable provided that it is performed for the benefit of the male voyeur and not its female participants.

An ordinary woman with plain old fashioned desires?

The image of Madonna constructed in the press casts her as an extremely manipulative woman capable of endangering social morals and values; a peddler of porn born of various traumatic events throughout her life, and, her consequent sexual confusion. However, in another vein the press simultaneously construct Madonna as being very ordinary and having ordinary and 'understandable' desires.

Attempting to expose the 'ordinariness' of Madonna's background and implicitly asking 'who does she think she is?' were numerous references to Madonna's real name. Misleadingly these imply that Madonna's stage name is entirely self appointed. None of the reports acknowledge that the singer was in fact christened by her parents with the first name of Madonna. The *Sunday Telegraph*, *Daily Star*, *Daily Mail*, *Daily Mirror* and *Daily Express* told readers that Madonna was, in reality, simply either Miss Ciccone, Louise Ciccone, Ms Louise Magdelena Ciccone or Louise Veronica Ciccone. The *Sunday Telegraph* added that she was 'the daughter of a Detroit car worker' and that 'she looks rather common'.[43] Madonna was not then born of royal blood. This becomes another explanation as to why Madonna exposed herself as she did in *Sex*: it was reflective of her low class origins. This stance is not surprising from the right-wing *Sunday Telegraph*. It is more surprising that this attitude toward an 'ordinary' person was adopted by the tabloid press. However, this illustrates Connell's view of the tabloid press that sometimes their

> populism is a sham. The most vitriolic of the attacks seems to be reserved for those who by good fortune have found themselves as one of the stars. They have not been born to stardom. It is, therefore, as if the tabloids are waiting for the inevitable, the moment when these parvenu personalities give themselves away and reveal the ordinariness of their origins.[44]

Writing about Madonna in this way, the papers make the point that although Madonna might think herself different to the rest of us she is in fact of just the same material. Connell argues that tabloid stories of this type are engaging in 'popular forms of political criticism' because they 'undermine the authority of those who place themselves apart. They encourage and nourish scepticism about the legitimacy of the class of personalities to act as they do.'[45] Certainly there is the suggestion that 'Louise Ciccone' has, in publishing *Sex*, taken the privileges granted by her fans too far.

Other means of establishing Madonna's 'ordinariness' claim to reveal the reality behind her facade. Fundamentally sexist, the arguments propounded are that Madonna is not the strong independent woman she would have us think. Rather, in reality (just like every woman) she is somewhat passive, needs a man to take care of her and/or, when it comes down to it, desires to have children.

Today offered an 'expert's' analysis of what lies behind Madonna's image. The 'expert' university psychologist concluded from a photograph of Madonna 'If someone was to ask me whether this was a strong person trying to look demure, or a demure person trying to look strong, I would say the latter.'[46] Drawing similar conclusions the *Sun* quoted Madonna as confiding to pop columnist Piers Morgan 'I'm just a lonely and insecure girl at heart and looking for a good looking intelligent man to dominate me.'[47] There is an indication that this revelation should not be taken too seriously. However, the adage that 'many a true word is spoken in jest' is certainly applied by the tabloids. When Madonna remarked to a man at the New York launch party of *Sex* that she wanted to have his baby, *Today* reported that it was 'a flippant comment that provided a clue to her innermost desires.'[48] Andrew Neil was of the same school of thought. When Madonna replied to a question concerning the possibility of her having children by saying 'it's an idea, sure', Neil concluded 'this was a far cry from her books and videos and films, but perhaps it is the real Madonna.'[49]

As with Marilyn Monroe, to whom at one time she was often compared, there is the strong suggestion that, after all, Madonna would most like to settle down and have a family and thereby find the love she never had as a child. It seems almost inconceivable to some that this is not the truth behind the facade. Thus, the image of the independent woman who is in control of her life and happy with it is only permitted to exist as a myth and not as a truthful expression of a woman's self.

So where lies the truth?

The image of Madonna constructed by the British press around the publication of *Sex* is complex and often highly contradictory. On the one hand Madonna is a manipulative self publicist of dubious sexuality using pornography for financial gain without concern for possible effects on young fans and society in general. On the other hand, and simultaneously, she is a confused and traumatized woman who wants to be part of a loving family unit. Many critical attacks upon Madonna simply do not add up when considered in terms of how the press itself operates: she is condemned for creating her own hype and seeking to make money when newspapers publish stories about stars for their own financial gain; she is criticized for exploiting pornography which the tabloid press are equally guilty of; and she is described as having lost her news value when the attention given to her by the press demonstrates that this is far from the case.

Although the image of Madonna constructed in the press and discussed here is a highly concentrated one, it does reveal the limited range of discourses through which the press process Madonna. In the vast majority of cases, these discourses are highly conservative in nature and reflective of male-dominated values, that seek to deny the validity of alternative sexualities or desires outside of the heterosexual. Critical emphasis is placed instead on Madonna as an individual. What is not discussed to any significant degree is the complexity of society and culture within which Madonna operates. The crucial issues of who controls imagery, texts and meanings in our society are ignored.

8 SEX:'Signed, Sealed, Delivered . . .'

Margery Metzstein

Madonna. Sex. These are the words running down the side of her cheek. Eyes closed, mouth open, nostrils flaring – an invitation to what? The Mylar bag crackles to the touch and satisfies a pre-genital need for sensation to provide several experiences simultaneously. The wrapper shimmers in seductive silver, reflecting the light, Madonna's image and the owner in a narcissistic bricolage. Carefully running a fingernail along the opening, suffused with excitement, the purchaser of *Sex*,[1] breathes in, and pulls out the contents.

This is not a book. The cover encodes a different message. The word *Sex* is etched in upper case in a sea of rippling aluminium, suggesting a pristine perfection. Pulling back the cover which promised so much produces a frisson of disappointment. The first page is brown paper, dull after so much silver, with the letters of Madonna and Sex interlinked, picked out in matt gold. The thrill has gone. Desire is a double edged sword. Afterwards you will realize that this is a package within a package, that the contents are enclosed in brown paper. This is a joke. The one about the man who went into a newsagents and bought a dirty magazine which came in a brown paper bag. Still, this is not a magazine either. It is a spiral bound collection of photographs and words printed on matt paper which imitates a more stylish, more expensive book of Art Photography by someone like Robert Mapplethorpe. The whole package comes complete with a CD of *Erotica*, which is wrapped in a mini Mylar re-sealable bag. This is illustrated with a design which suggests a vagina, enclosing an X which presumably marks the spot. The letters of the word EROTIC run across the centre of the X. Get it? The postmodern packaging, the knowing puns, the sly jokes, all suggest the more recent, self reflexive world of advertising, where pop music and the product jostle for significance amidst a welter of disconnected signs which all proclaim: Buy Me. Like Magritte's pipe, *ceci n'est pas un livre*.

It is an invitation to own a piece of Madonna; her ass and her 'intimate' fantasies. The Queen of desire is selling desire which can never be fulfilled. That is the point of this product which slid into the world, symbiotically tied to the media which self-interestedly promoted both itself and this bastard child of 'the culture industry'.

As David Tetzlaff points out in *The Madonna Connection*,[2] it is not that Madonna can be accused of being a 'sellout', it is rather 'that Madonna's conscious self-commodification may be the primary trait for which she is admired by her mainstream audience.' From this point of view, consumers of *Sex* will have much to admire since in this package Madonna nakedly sells her image on almost every available surface. This makes her previous marketing strategies seem modest by comparison. It is not particularly surprising that Madonna has co-opted sex as a further marketing ploy since her sexuality is a facet of her appeal or, from another point of view, of her hard sell. For she has always primarily promoted herself above anything else – packaged variously in different phases of her career but nonetheless selling herself rather than, for example, her songwriting, singing or dancing abilities. It is her capacity continually to re-create herself, normally a positive process but in her case hollow, which causes ambivalence in the response of feminists and some of her fans, while being the main 'secret of her success'. On the one hand, it is difficult to dispute that Madonna is a powerful woman, in control of her affairs, and as such can be seen as a positive role model for women. On the other, as *Forbes* magazine commented: 'Madonna wants rigid control of her own publicity', and being a shrewd businesswoman might be incompatible with the 'naughty' image she has so carefully crafted. The point is not that Madonna makes a lot of money, nor that her version of sexuality is particularly crass – not at any rate compared to Stallone and Schwarzenegger, who both trade on a crude stereotyped masculinity – but that she is reluctant to discuss this aspect of her talent. This is interesting because it indicates a remarkably traditional perspective on the relationship between art and commerce which harks back to a crude version of Romantic dualism. Does Madonna think that her status as an 'artist' would be compromised, tainted, if she is associated with filthy lucre? *Forbes* imply that the disassociation effected between her art and her business abilities is part of Madonna's astuteness as a businesswoman. However, judging from her *Newsweek* interview it is clear that she has imbibed a confused notion of the artist through a jumbled set of discourses which still circulate in our culture. These have filtered through from the language of 'High Art' via Hollywood biopics – just think of those fabulous kitsch 'portraits of the artist' like Kirk Douglas as Van Gogh – or the language of Rock/Pop speak apparent in those excruciating interviews with rock and pop stars, wittily parodied in the film *Spinal*

Stargazing. The US launch party for *Sex*.

Tap. When asked by David Ansen, the *Newsweek* interviewer, if *Sex* will 'change people's attitudes', Madonna replies:

> I think that it can start the machinery going for change. I do in a way see myself as a revolutionary at this point.[3]

This statement suggests that Madonna is aligning herself with the *avant garde* artist, in the vanguard of a new movement for sexual liberation which her public will eventually embrace. Even the name of her persona, Dita Parlo, adopted for *Sex* suggests an affinity with the avant garde, since the latter is the name of the actress who plays Juliette in Jean Vigo's 1934 film, *L'Atalante*. Vigo was a director whose techniques and subject matter had links with surrealist artists. Madonna has borrowed not only Dita Parlo's name but has also mimicked her appearance, her hairstyle and make-up – although she has introduced a severity of style which is reminiscent of the more androgynous look of Marlene Dietrich. However, these hints at links with the avant garde are nothing more than Madonna's regurgitation of images and ideas evident in other areas of her work. Further on in the *Newsweek* interview she changes her discourse from that of sexual revolutionary to sexual relativist:

> Look; everybody has different needs and wants and preferences and desires and fantasies. And we should not damn somebody or judge somebody because it's different than yours.[4]

Very fine sentiments but certainly not revolutionary nor avoiding cliché. This relativism strikingly avoids the issue of power and begins to sound closer to Spinal Tap's Nigel Tuffnell than André Breton. As Tuffnell says about a piece of music he has composed, 'I'm really influenced by Mozart and Bach and it's sort of in between those. It's like a Mach piece.'[5] Similarly, the Madonna school of sexual liberation presents itself as bringing 'subversive ideas about sexuality into the mainstream'.[6] This sounds like a cross between Havelock Ellis and Dr Ruth, whom it could be argued is more subversive. Another problem with these sentiments, noted by *Newsweek*, is that they are:

> uncharacteristically redundant. Throughout her career, Madonna has thrived by embracing underground night club subcultures and taking them mainstream. This time, she's behind the curve. Sex is already out there in the light.[7]

This is another way of saying that her Mylar bagged fantasies are desperately uncool, which must be worrying if you're a street-cred junkie. However, I want to focus on the problems arising from Madonna's sexual relativism which are signalled in the text of *Sex*.

On the matt brown paper which frames the contents, Madonna once again demonstrates the dualism which seems to underpin much of her thinking:

> THIS BOOK IS ABOUT SEX. SEX IS NOT LOVE. LOVE IS NOT SEX. BUT THE BEST OF BOTH WORLDS IS CREATED WHEN THEY COME TOGETHER.

This separation between sex and love seems to be necessary to her project, which is to suggest that sex can inhabit a pure fantasy realm, disconnected from the world, where anything you can imagine can safely take place without repercussions. While this might be true of fantasy unexpressed, it is not true of *Sex*, which is circulating in the world and as such cannot be disowned as a fiction. The desire to separate sex from love, truth from fiction, fantasy from reality, is one which underpins the text and appears to be an elaborate disclaimer. Madonna seems to want it all ways. Yes *this* is about sex, but I believe in love. Sure these are my fantasies, but they are not real and finally this is fiction so don't be stupid enough to confuse what appears here with the truth about what I do, which I'm not telling you anyway. As in her videos, Madonna wants to dance into view, shake her tailfeather and dance off screen unscathed, and untouched by any of the consequences which her publication might have stirred up. Marina Warner, writing in *The Observer*, points out some of the difficulties with Madonna's dualism in *Sex*:

> Part of the revolution in sensibility which finds a figurehead in Madonna wants women to thrive on a radical break between sex and love: it recasts ideas about women and their erotic drives to make them more like truckers in topless bars or specialist gays in S&M groups.[8]

This seems to be the main drive behind *Sex*. Enclosed within the aluminium covers are photographs which show Madonna caught in the act of various forms of, what she supposes to be, marginalized sexual relationships. 'I'll teach you how to fuck' runs the slogan accompanying a picture of Madonna, dressed in a black leather-studded bikini with peek-a-boo nipples, black leather mask and wristbands. She is sucking one middle finger and touching her crotch with the other. Madonna as mistress of ceremonies waits for us to turn the page and join her in a feast of polymorphous perversity. Well, not quite. Instead we have a procession of posed, stylized tableaux which bear a striking resemblance to Steven Meisel's earlier work for Italian *Vogue*. Meisel, who is responsible for Madonna's photographs in *Sex*, appears in the tenth anniversary edition of *The Face*, which also features Madonna.[9] A selection of Meisel's photographs appear and include the models Naomi Campbell and Isabella Rossellini, the former of whom is shown naked in a pool with Christy Turlington, an S&M theme and a harshly lit street scene which are all repeated in *Sex*. The selection of black leather outfits in *Sex* could indeed be adverts for Jon Richmond, Pam Hogg or a number of other designers who sport with an S&M theme. Each photograph strikes a pose. Madonna 'voguing' with lesbians, bound and gagged, knife held to her crotch. Madonna in S&M scene; with legs in the air; with fetishists; younger men; gay men; or sucking a toe. Madonna lying back on a fur rug, trousers undone, smoking a post coital cigarette, looking like a reject from *Fiesta* magazine. Then there is winsome Madonna, sucking a child-like thumb, covered in a pattern of reflected light – a moment's respite perhaps from the hard fucking she has supposedly been through. More action. Madonna with a dog; in a gay bar, watching and encouraging. Madonna as Marilyn Monroe, hair caught in cute little bunches. Madonna's crotch beavering across the centre page, body captured in a mutilated pose as if headless, and largely limb-less. Madonna masturbating over a mirror; with older man; on the beach with Isabella Rossellini, clad in gold *lame* shorts with Vanilla Ice; naked on the highway, or simulating sex against a tree. Madonna sandwiched between Big Daddy Kane and Naomi Campbell imitating an oreo biscuit – the name of which is a term of abuse for a 'white negro', an uncle Tom, because it's black on the outside and white inside. Another pause, another moment of quiet reflection, with Madonna looking out of a window, while absentmin-dedly touching her ass – this is, incidentally the best photograph in the collection because at least here she looks engaged. A few more shots follow of Madonna alone, then cut to a petrol station where she plays, topless, with a pump, cut to naked in a pizza bar, eating a pizza, cut to sleazy strip joints and Madonna as street walker, cut to a chair with whips. Fade.

As the repeated use of the name Madonna should suggest, these photographs are all about Madonna looking good. She surrounds herself with a group of mostly unprepossessing models in what Zoe Heller calls 'a nasty sort of aesthetic facism'.[10] This is not subvers-ive, it's not about sex, it's about Madonna's ultimate 'self commodi-fication'. What a great ploy; her image circulating throughout the world and at $50 per copy as well. She has nothing to sell here but herself – the black leather, the whips and the people are all extras in the Big Con. As Warren Beatty comments in *In Bed with Madonna*:

> She doesn't want to live off camera. There's nothing to say. Why would you say something if it's off camera?[11]

Even her separation between sex and love, her sexual libertarianism, is a huge ploy. Everything is grist to her mill. She recycles any discourse which can aid her ultimate goal, which is always to sell herself, using anything which comes to hand. Language, leather, Catholicism, rape, homosexuals, lesbians, blacks, Hispanics; it doesn't really matter as long as she homes in on the target audience. Near the end of *Sex*, there is a brief dialogue above the photographs of sleazy strip joints which runs:

> Doctor: Have you ever been mistaken for a prostitute?
> Dita: Everytime anyone reviews anything I do, I'm mistaken for a prostitute.

If prostitution is defined as someone who sells themselves for money, or someone who degrades themselves by publicity, then this is the correct word to describe Madonna. When my daughter and her friends were looking through *Sex*, my eleven-year-old son walked into her bedroom and caught a glimpse of the contents. He started to cry. Later, when I asked why he was crying he said:

> She doesn't need to show herself like that. She's got lots of money already. She just wants to be popular. She's a sad, sad person.

He realized, even if we adults do not – with our sophisticated theoretical rationalizations – that this book is an insult which degrades Madonna, and humiliates women. A culture which can easily accommodate its own degradation is terminally ill. This has been said before, most notably by Horkheimer and Adorno in *Dialectic of Enlightenment*,[12] published in 1944. Their chapter on 'The Culture Industry' painstakingly tracks the relationships created in a society in which 'the basis on which technology acquires power over society is the power of those whose economic hold over society is greatest.' This means that mass culture, which includes the entertainment industry, feeds off both icons and consumers which it creates. Those who own the technology on which mass culture relies also own the individual in the sense that 'the need which might resist central control has already been suppressed by the control of the individual consciousness.' Madonna is from this point of view no more than another pawn in the game whose position is only different in degree, but not in kind, from that of her audience. Both Madonna and audience are necessary participants in a process which impoverishes all and creates the promise of fulfilment which can never be delivered. *Sex* is the perfect metaphor for this process because everyone is being fucked, including those who think they are doing the fucking. S&M is a more specific summation of the process because it emphasizes the symbiotic nature of the relationship and the violence caused to the spirit of the, willing or unwilling, participants. If this kind of analysis is open to the charge of pessimism then at least I'm in good company. I wept with my son because I recognized my own reaction which had previously been buried under layers of accommodation.

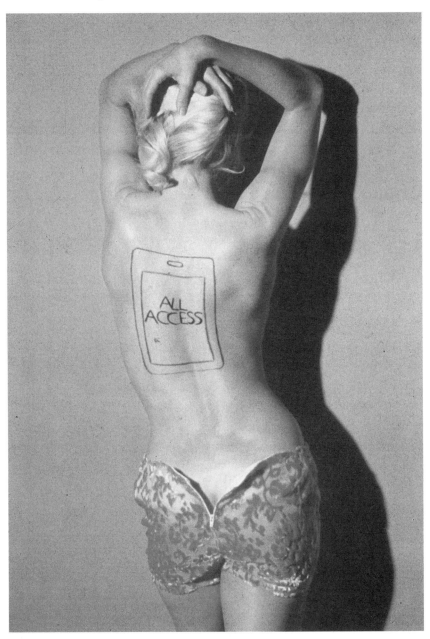

Madonna, by Steve Meisel.

9 Rights and Permissions: *Sex*, the Model and the Star

Sue Wiseman

I

One of the issues raised by *Sex* and other nude photographs of Madonna is the question: 'Who can look at whom and what does it "mean"?' Rather than pursue these issues using the binary terms posed by the debate about pornography and censorship (terms which could be argued to be mutually reinforcing in their very assumption of precise opposition) I want to pose the question of how the roles of model and star coincide with or contradict one another. I shall place this in relation to the way in which the viewer is invited to use the photograph in terms of scenario, form, content, character, framing. In doing this I will be using the terms 'aesthetic' and 'pornography' in a particular way not to refer to the actions represented in an image in terms of obscenity or morality, but to the reading context which invites or implies a particular kind of response. A large part of how we read an image is circumstantial and *Sex*, like other images and texts, invites a different kind of response according to context.[1]

It is a commonplace in journalism and criticism of Madonna that she is interested in power and control, but it is an even more widely acknowledged commonplace that in the traditions of painting and photography of the female body, the model is in a relatively powerless position. However gymnastic her ability to pose, the female model has been construed as the 'raw' material shaped by creativity and composition into the painting. In contemporary critical semiotics too, the model is seen as part of a stage preceding representation, excluded from critical analysis because whatever she did is excluded once again from analysis of the sign – beyond the recoverable context of the painting or photographic text. The part played by the model remains largely untheorized and mysterious.[2] The star, on the other hand, while also a model when posed in photographs, is situated by critical discourse in a narrative of increasing control – film histories repeatedly tell of the place of the star in the struggles for power and money in the film business.[3]

There are obvious tensions between these two ways of seeing the figure – the female model creatively if not physically inert, transformed into art by the gaze of the creator, versus the female star manipulating a sequence of images and constantly promising – or threatening – to generate meanings which overpower the framework within which she has been placed. With the model, we are invited to think about the overall composition, not to speculate on character or narrative concerned with any figure beyond the image. With the star, the implications of the figure move between the implications of the image 'itself' – which as soon as the viewer knows the subject is a star ceases to exist 'in itself' – and extra-imagistic implications associated with the star. We have all had the experience of seeing a photograph and then being told that it is a famous person. At such a moment the meaning of the image changes.

This ability of context and time to change meanings generated by texts has particular implications for nude photography, where the tradition of posing models and star photography coincide. The nude or 'girlie' pictures of a star are not model photographs (where the viewer is invited to concentrate on making meaning from the picture not the 'character' of the figure) because the star-model immediately seems to have control over the circumstances. Nor are they star personality photographs. They move between the two. For example, in the case of *Sex*, the control exerted by the star/model is coded into the relationship between pictures and text. But the whole issue of the 'meanings' of the female figure in the photograph – the contradictory meanings of model versus star – cuts across and troubles a sequence of other debates and binary distinctions where each category 'ensures' the other one, crucially the mutually dependent oppositions between the 'pornographic' and the 'artistic'.

II

The question of these two crucial and assumed oppositions between model/star and 'artistic'/'pornographic' is raised explicitly in relation to Madonna by the gloriously named Martin Hugo Maximilian Schreiber, who had the luck to photograph Madonna in 1979 – when she was a 'mere' model. Against Madonna's will he capitalized on his good fortune when his model became a famous star and published *Madonna: Nudes 1979*. Before the photographs, Schreiber's book reproduces a form headed 'Model Release' – presumably published to prove that, legally, he did indeed have control over the photographs of his now famous subject in all positions and aesthetic orders from abstract to split beaver. The form gives us a very helpful legal definition of the model in photography:

> I hereby give [Martin H. Schreiber] the absolute right and permission to copyright and/or publish, or use photographic portraits or pictures of me, or in which I may be included in the whole or in part, or composite or distorted in character or form, in conjunction with my

own or a fictitious name, or reproductions thereof in colour or other-wise, made through any media at his studios or elsewhere, for art, advertising or any other lawful purpose whatsoever.

I hereby waive any right that I may have to inspect and/or approve the finished product or the advertising copy that may be used in connection therewith, or the use to which it may be applied.[4]

The legal position of the model articulated here coincides to a large extent with the aesthetic understanding of the model as raw material out of which the creator makes art. The model signs away not only the right to control her whole body in verisimilar representation but in *any* part or under *any* aesthetic – this legal document specifies the 'absolute right' of the creator in the model-artist relation. Legally, this relationship is the same whatever product the photographer produces. Indeed, the contract seems to be specifically designed to cover *both* 'artistic' and 'pornographic' representations using the model.

At precisely this point the legal understanding of the body of the model parts company from the traditional aesthetic understanding of the opposition of the female nude to pornography. The female nude, as Lynda Nead's recent study elucidates, is problematic for critics because of its potential sensual appeal – it troubles the very high-art tradition of which it forms the apotheosis. As Nead puts it, 'More than any other subject, the female nude connotes "Art" . . . how does the image of the female body displayed in an art gallery relate to other images of the female body produced within mass culture?'[5] The nudes in Schreiber's *Madonna: Nudes 1979* enable us to recognize that alongside the culturally understood compositional codes (such as posing, captioning, intertextuality with and quo-tation from or reference to other images or photographic styles) the status of any particular photograph in relation to high art or porno-graphy is changed and created by the context within which it is read. Madonna becoming a star is one of the contexts which has changed the cultural implications and value of these 1979 photo-graphs. They were reproduced in the 1980s in *Playboy* – at that time the most respectable end of the men's pornography market. But it was known that they were reproduced against the will of the now famous subject and constituted a prying into her past rather than a free engagement with the camera in the present – like Monroe's or Loren's willing star poses for American *Esquire* in the fifties and sixties. In 1993 the photographs themselves show Madonna, (in 1979 they showed a model) partly clothed, unclothed, with a cat, and progress to images of her on all fours imitating the pose of a 'hungry pussy'. Iconographically, such visual associations and half coy puns put them at a border between 'good taste' shots inviting a notionally disinterested artistic gaze, and pornography. They could be posed for *Playboy* or pop posters which use some of the same images, transformed by the different contexts of, say, a teenager's wall versus presence in a masturbation magazine.

Schreiber's foreword in attempting to make the case for his nudes of Madonna as non-sensual, high-culture images helpfully delineates some of the issues in the debate about the borders of pornography – both in relation to a 'model' in subservient poses who has now become a star. He attempts to make sense of what 'his' images now mean – are they of a model, or of 'Madonna'? And where do they stand, therefore, in relation to the 'art'/'porn' divide?

> In September 1985 *Playboy* magazine published four of my photographs of Madonna. I was proud to have those images published and to share the pages with a great museum photographer, a contemporary, Lee Friedlander. We are both serious 'art photographers', an important distinction, and I felt that made the nudes not only more acceptable, but placed them on a higher level. They were nude studies, devoid of prurient interests, having nothing to do with sex or exploitation and that is just how they should be viewed. I say this because, unfortunately, a lot of people want to see or believe something else. Nudes have been in art for centuries. We are fascinated by the human form, by our bodies and that fascination won't stop. There are those who would like it otherwise, who would like to 'sully', make dirty the image of nudes.
>
> This book is a celebration of the human form, a dedication to an innocent, determined, young woman and to all figure models. (Foreword, np)

While the legal contract conflates the model for art and porn, the photographer's argument emphasizes the importance and true existence of the boundary between the two, and suggests that his photographs of Madonna sustain rather than disrupt that boundary because they use her body for – *art*. But what distinguishes the way in which a viewer looks at these two categories? And why does Schreiber present himself as anxious to preserve his images from that kind of viewing which might 'sully' art photography? He asserts that he is an 'art photographer', in response to an imagined counter-claim that he is a pornographer. He cannot prove his case from the images themselves – because of their poses and iconography and importantly because as nude photographs they participate in one of the dominant pornographic modes. Moreover, the context of publication in 1990 must include the interest of the viewer in seeing the star, Madonna, with her kit off.

Schreiber's foreword is confused by the fact that what was once 'his' model has become a star and a star body is not, in his own aesthetic, suitable as artistic raw material or pornography. Thus, the boundary of art/porn for his photographers is doubly troubled – once by the poses and the *Playboy* context which suggests that his disclaimer is disingenuous, and again by the transformation of a model into a star. Although Madonna was not in control of the content of the pictures people were not buying Schreiber's art-photography but Madonna – nude. While the republication of these pictures demonstrates the transformation of the significance of Madonna's body wrought by stardom, it also exposes the problematic negotiation between a disinterested artistic gaze and a sensual or pornographic engagement with the text. As Lynda Nead points out, the female nude itself tests the terms of the distinction between art and obscenity because it is 'not only at the centre of the definition of art, but also on the edge of the category, pushing against the limit, brushing against obscenity'. This is both appropriate and inappropriate for the 'artistic' gaze that Schreiber invokes.[6]

In different ways, both *Sex* and *Madonna: Nudes 1979* bring up the problem of how to look at a nude or an obscene photograph in relation to the body of the star. The privileged category of the 'artistic' way of looking can be seen as operating in distinction to a pornographic/masturbatory gaze. The acquisition of artistic looking gives the viewer what Bourdieu sees as cultural capital.[7] Schreiber's claims attempt to keep 'his' images pure, though through Madonna's stardom they have waywardly come to be in some extra-legal sense 'her' images. *Sex* presents itself as the star's body staged in an erotic exploration of categories traditionally considered at the fashionable borders of the 'obscene' in representation and classified as pornography.[8]

More importantly, Madonna, having pursued a relatively traditional career moving from model to star, *returns* in *Sex* to a discourse in which models are the subject only in a very limited sense (as 'desire', one might say). For want of a better term *and* because the iconography of *Sex* insists on the book's participation in this discourse, this must be called the pornographic. In returning to 'porn', Madonna locates her fame and stardom in or against the discourse which is understood as requiring 'models' and producing 'models' in scenarios, not stars. Does this return imply that the star once again becomes a model? The initial images are within the iconographic traditions of pornography. And one message in the introduction and implied by the range of sexual activities represented is: anything goes between consenting adults (but only some things are nice to look at – fat is 'a big problem'). All kinds of sex are condoned in the foreword: 'Sex is not love. Love is not sex . . . But the best way for human beings to show love is to love one

another.' Thus the book presents itself as a kind of annexation of soft-porn values and sensibility to a 'permissive' ethic under the twin signs of beauty and safety/consent. However, text and image work together closely in this case because we know that the book is 'by' Madonna. Although Steven Meisel took the photographs, she was model, designer, setter of the scene – and she had control over the captions and text.[9]

Indeed the authoritative voice of the star opens the text. 'This book does not condone unsafe sex. These are fantasies I have dreamed up. Like most human beings, when I let my mind wander, when I let myself go, I rarely think of condoms. My fantasies take place in a perfect world, a place without AIDS. Unfortunately, the world is not perfect and I know that condoms are not only necessary but mandatory.' This disclaimer, while it fits in with Madonna's widely publicized sensible attitude to HIV and condoms, also points to the range of aesthetics operating within the book as drawing on and utilizing pornographic visual codes to the extent that they do not permit the disruptive entry of safe sex issues into the visual images themselves. The articulation of the need for safe sex frames the invitation to fantasy but is not allowed to interrupt the reader's enjoyment of the fantasies as far as the visual material is concerned. This disclaimer is the first indication that the relationship of text to photograph is not simply corroborative. Other issues are invited into the text next to the pictures.

There is a photograph of a bestockinged and bodystockinged Madonna in a club setting, bent backwards on a machine called 'Taxi' decorated with Santa Claus and with a television screen hanging over her as a leather clad man supports her backside. The accompanying discourse is an exchange between 'Dita' and 'Doctor' on 'ass-fucking', but our gaze is concentrated on the inside of Madonna's left thigh, not her anus. 'Dita' explains the pleasures of ass-fucking. It turns out that as well as being an exquisite combination of pleasure and pain, it is a real problem: 'if you're not excited, or if you're not doing it right, things can go really wrong.' So: be careful boys and girls. Here is a discursive shift from an image inviting diverse fantasy to descriptive and didactic captioning. First, the image itself is ambiguous about what it could be presenting. We are not looking, exactly, at ass-fucking. Then, while inviting us to think about ass-fucking and thereby to an extent captioning the photographic image as 'showing' this, the written text shifts from pleasure to consent, from fantasy to practicality, insisting on consent and care. So, where the aesthetic of the photograph draws

Taking the wraps off *Sex*.

on soft porn with a hint of more specialized leather interest, the written text shifts register from an insistence on pleasure to assume the tone of a caring 'how-to' guide.

At other points, too, non- or even anti-erotic discourses are inserted as commentary: the disquisition on fat; a series of lectures on the meaning of bondage and the relationship between bondage and rich women who stay in abusive relationships; a discourse on women and porn videos. None of these offer masturbatory fantasies to the reader, pointing rather to the complexities of economic and social conditions which underlie the images presented for fantasy. The value of what the lectures have to say about these issues is another question – their value is as the 'star's opinion'.

Such didactic interludes cannot be taken in precisely the same way as photographs and scenarios with the rubric of fantasy 'I made it all up' given at the beginning. After all, they present themselves as social commentary as well as explicatory captions. One of the most evident examples of the captions and commentary forming a counterpoint rather than simply reinforcing the images occurs during the early bondage and domination sequence when the text permits itself to point back to a putative original experience which the fantasy/photograph reworks. A fairly small image shows a leather-man strapping a Madonna leg to chains, while the text tells us that being tied up has 'something comforting' in it: 'Like when you were a baby and your mother strapped you in the car seat'. The image *presents* the fantasy while the text *explicates* it by offering an instant analysis of an 'original situation' which the fantasy re-enacts. Many psychiatric practitioners do work within these terms. But, crucially, therapists – normative or otherwise – are involved in analysing rather than inviting fantasy.

Thus, at various points, *Sex* allows itself the textual liberty of using captioning to disrupt the very act it is presenting. This offers clues to the way in which the text while presenting itself as within a pornographic aesthetic (emphatically foregrounded in the provocative opening with images of lesbian S&M, an issue at the core of many feminist debates around pornography and censorship) is in fact also operating in terms of the star persona and body. So what *are* the implications of a star using pornographic poses?

Sex appears to be making a claim to be pornography and to be showing the body in attitudes and activities considered 'perverse'. It initially presents a reader-viewer with a clearly stated erotic/pornographic aesthetic. But not only is the text organized backwards in relation to the traditional masturbatory text in that it moves from 'hard' to 'soft' images, but in terms of visual style it also moves from a porn aesthetic to more jokey and abstract/surreal modes of representation. For example, the images of Madonna with props such as cigarettes, handbags, bunny tails and high sandals might echo feminist commentaries on femininity at the same time as suggesting themselves as material for the elaboration of fantasy. Even as the visual images invite the erotic/pornographic gaze in a very overt way (open legs, girl looking in mirror pushing up breasts, girl masturbating over mirror, girl exposing herself at window, girl almost naked in rich private garden) some also make claims to self-consciousness. If we want to we can read the visual style in terms of their relationship to Renaissance images of Venus, the work of Man Ray and the contemporary photographers who interrogate sexuality such as Robert Mapplethorpe and Cindy Sherman.

Robert Mapplethorpe's photographs of male and female bodybuilders play on the interrelationship of the athletic/beautiful body and the question of obscenity. This was presented most forcefully by Mapplethorpe in his images of homosexual eroticism which, by remaining enigmatic point out the problem of how such photographs are looked at – whether sensually or 'artistically'. Mapplethorpe emphasizes the sense of the body as classically beautiful – a value to some extent shared between photographic texts which could be posed at the most extreme end of the high art and pornographic oppositions. But because of the content of the images being coded in themselves as 'obscene' versus their overtly artistic control they tend to re-pose the problem of reading.[10]

While Mapplethorpe's photographs offer the reader a binary though not necessarily resoluble choice between artistic and obscene looking, the photographs of Cindy Sherman – both in the early *Film Stills* and in the more recent colour images – take the ingredients of the picture which invite either the aesthetic or the sensual gaze and rearrange them in ways which trouble and render visible the way in which the two categories are uncoded. Although she does not usually work with nudes, her images often call attention to the particular props and codes which support the staging of the female body as for the gaze within the framework of either the aesthetic or the erotic. Where *Sex* banishes condoms, one Sherman image arranges them in various states of foldedness and use, one with a sausage in it on a tablecloth, others folded as one might find them under the bed – parodying the underside of the gaze invited in the erotic framing. Sherman is in the photograph too because, as we have been told, she uses herself as the model for her photographs. She has become, in a way, the endlessly disguised star of her 'film' stills. *Sex*, as well as using Mapplethorpe's concentration on muscle and outline – and the question of aesthetic versus obscene – could also be seen as using some of the techniques which Sherman uses to pose the question for the viewer of how we are accustomed to look at the female figure.[11]

Even as Madonna's body models the scenes she is in control of them – they are *her* photographs not the photographer's, whatever he brings to the staging and lighting. In its multitude of poses and scenes the whole text is authorised by the star name – Madonna. So the volume is both a collection of staged scenes, moments, fantasies, narratives and a sequence of shots of the star, Madonna, as stills would be of a star actress. However, the moments of direct address (when the voice of the text lectures or explains not as 'Dita' but in 'the Voice of Madonna') make it clear that the text is not authored by the discourse of pornography or art, which – crucially – speak from positions of enunciation distinct from and even distant from the model. This text runs together the position of enunciation and the model for it is 'Madonna', who gives us permission to see her in these poses which she herself has made. Perhaps the closest analogy is with posed film star stills or publicity shots (which sometimes show scenes that do not actually take place in the film, but suggest others which do). In this case the shots are of the guises assumed by the star Madonna. She has absolute rights over the image and we are permitted to see her transforming and reinventing herself. We are *allowed* to look, by the model who also controls the pictures.

III

Sex's sense of star authorisation can gel only problematically with the pornographic horizon of expectation instantiated by the text's opening visual style. *Sex* presents itself as pornography but because the model is also the locus of enunciation (the source of the text), we can ask again – is it possible for star stills to enter fully into the discourse of the pornographic? Taking up Richard Dyer's point about the charisma of a star, it seems that under the aegis of a star the context of poses associated with the 'obscene' is indeed trans-formed as a play of cultural meanings.[12] By which I do not mean that Madonna alters taste and morality for better or worse by using lesbian and gay images. Rather, I would suggest that whenever Madonna is framed as allowing herself to be seen in a particular action, the energy of the image is channelled like lightning into the significance of her stardom. Where such images might indeed be used for masturbatory fantasy, the star presence is always the central issue.

The book's wide embrace of marketable sexual fantasies means

'I'm tired of being compared to Marilyn Monroe'.

that within the realm of what 'can be shown' the text appears liberal – it can be read as liberating women's fantasy, as concentrating on women's pleasure, as offering in equal status heterosexual and same-sex representations or, alternatively, as exploiting real differences by annexing all images to marketability for a mass audience. In this sense it is an open text, positively inviting commentary in a way that *Playboy* does not. But where it is not open is in the presiding genius of the star.

The force, political implications, and excitement – as well, perhaps, as what some would find the offensiveness, of Madonna's poses and implied actions in *Sex* is put at one remove from the pornographic discourse it seeks to enter (and perhaps desires to transform). The controlling presence of the star renders every fist fuck analogous to other images of the Madonna-star, like the self conscious quotation of a film still or publicity shot. For the book to achieve 'obscenity' we would have to forget Madonna. However, the control of Madonna-star over these representations, and her active choice of pornographic imagery and narrative for her self-preservation reverses the familiar career path from artistic or pornographic model to film or other stardom. Madonna's choice of pornographic imagery for her stills does not produce a pornographic text in the same sense that *Playboy* might be considered to be.

Epilogue: Acrostics[1]

Kathleen McHugh

Media, especially electronic media, change almost everything about what and how we know. They alter not only
our access to knowledge, but the very character and structure of that knowledge. Electronic media yield a cognitive
system wherein information is immediate, overabundant,
and increasingly diversionary. I use this last term both in its
sense of something that deflects, turns aside, and distracts,
as well as its meanings related to entertainment and amusement.
Media 'flow' is structurally and economically averse to getting to the
point. Its function is transmission rather than arrival at closure or
truth. Consequently, instead of being organized conceptually, analytically, or generically, in terms of the subject matter it transmits,
media knowledge is often assembled according to the capacities and
format of the technologies and the economies involved in transmit-
ting that material. When the US went to war in the Persian Gulf,
concerned American citizens following the conflict found themselves
immersed in a media extravaganza in which lines between news and
drama and between different electronic modes were blurred. TV
news reportage of air raids depicted the control panels and tracking
devices in US bombers zeroing in on their targets, giving viewers
images not unlike those customarily seen on the screens of video
games. The point-of-view camera position afforded the TV viewer
the same abstracted perspective of actual bombings as crews flying
the bombers. It looked like a game. Elaborate computer generated
graphics heralded news updates entitled 'A Line in the Sand' or,
more prosaically, 'War in the Gulf'. The interactional capacities of
electronic media, their global reach and immediacy, also help to
render them highly self-reflexive. Again, the conflict in the Middle
East serves as an excellent example. The Persian Gulf was a war in
which questions about who was watching CNN and issues concerning media coverage were considered as important as casualty
reports, if not more so. It would be difficult, if not impossible, to
talk about this war without talking about the media. But I use the
war as a very accessible, very dramatic example of the symptoms of
this electronic knowledge system. If my subject is actually the
'material' girl, then the material of which she is made is media. Like
the war, it is difficult to discuss her without discussing electronic
knowledge – its allusive, tangential and structurally superficial qua-

lities. Rather than directly addressing my subject, I would like to avoid her, and let my material, my commentary emulate the quality of hers.

An anecdote illustrates one of the problems involved in talking about her in the theoretical ways in which I have been trained. While a graduate student, I participated in a lecture series on topics in cultural studies, and I remember one of the events rather well for the ways in which it failed. Many of the students who gathered for a talk entitled 'Masculinity and *Miami Vice*' were freshmen; so many of them, we had to open up another, much larger room to accommodate the crowd. This group was unusual in its composition as all the other talks had drawn graduate students and faculty, but no freshmen. Later we learned that at this university, freshmen taking speech classes were required to attend and report on five talks given on campus during the semester. They had seen *Miami Vice* in the title and were drawn to its familiarity and accessibility. As the person handling the video equipment, I ended up in the back of the room; my reception of the paper included the reactions of the young students to the dense theoretical discourse it contained. The speaker made use of Lacan to articulate a thesis involving masculinity and spectacle. The students, who began by taking notes, soon ceased, their backs bending over the desks, their bodies drooping. Midway through the talk, the speaker showed a clip that depicted Sonny Crockett and Ricardo Tubbs talking aggressively to a drug dealer sitting in a sleek and shiny black car. The background music became louder as the conversation drew to an end, and the car screeched off in a crescendo of gut-throbbing disco rock. During the clip, the students sat up, they tapped their feet. The talk continued, and the undergraduates drifted out of the room one by one. When the speaker was finished, I had two questions. First, I wondered how or even if critical theoretical discourse could borrow or steal the allure and the accessibility of popular culture texts without succumbing to their banality.[2] Second, I wondered why and how the shallow superficiality of the *Miami Vice* clip reduced the very articulate theoretical argument contained in the talk to rubble.

Depth and surface – the discursive incompatibility that characterized this talk bears mention only because it was the TV show that undermined the theory and not vice-versa. Many contemporary thinkers have noted that western conceptions of knowledge are based on questionable dichotomies that privilege 'truth' (the profound, ideal, general and essential) and disparage 'appearance' (the superficial, actual, particular and trivial). These dichotomies have obvious ideological consequences, in that marginalized groups (e.g.

women, persons of colour) are often equated with the latter characteristics, while a white male perspective is hidden within the former.
While this encounter between the popular and the theoretical did
not disrupt these affiliations,[3] it did alter their customary hierarchical positions. The superficial threatened and levelled the profound.

One provocative narrative that concretizes the incompatibilities
between a theoretical perspective and the popular comes from
Michel de Certeau. He tells a New York story, a parable about
viewing the city from atop the World Trade Center. Of the hypothe-
tical urban spectator, he says:

> His elevation transforms him into a voyeur. It puts him at a distance.
> It transforms the bewitching world by which one was 'possessed' into
> a text that lies before one's eyes. It allows one to read it, to be a solar
> Eye, looking down like a god. The exaltation of a scopic and gnostic
> drive: the fiction of knowledge is related to this lust to be a viewpoint
> and nothing more.[4]

Distance and elevation characterize 'the voyeur-god', whose
position affords him or her the ability to see the extent and limits of
the city below. This perspective – one which de Certeau asserts,
produces a 'theoretical' account of the city – makes it impossible to
grasp or fathom the everyday practices that make up the invisible
lives on the streets.[5] What I am interested in here is the assertion
that the theoretical view is an elevated and distanced one, a view-
point that is predicated upon (a belief in) depth, substance, and
sufficient distance to bring the totality, the contours, of any phenomenon into view. The voyeur-god does not participate, does not
touch or mingle, does not tap his or her feet. As de Certeau remarks,
this eye, this gaze is associated with the fiction of knowledge, with
the position of the one who knows. It is a contemplative eye trained
most recently upon the film screen. Where the voyeuristic gaze and
situation of the film spectator was very compatible with psychoana-
lytic theory, especially the Lacanian semiotic model, the televisual
technologies that have succeeded the cinema solicit a different kind
of gaze (a 'glance', according to John Ellis[6]). To theorize these
technologies and their subjects in a manner that takes account of a
very different look, different pleasures, and different structures of
knowledge might demand a different sort of critical discourse.

Not all contemporary approaches to media attempt to theorize their
textuality – a term that refers here to the points of intersection
between texts, language, and subjectivity – based on the structure of
the texts themselves. While semiotic psychoanalysis has attempted
to diagnose such points, cultural studies focuses on audiences. As

Ien Ang defines the field, it aims 'to arrive at a more historicized insight into the ways in which "audience activity" is related to social and political structures and processes.'[7] For her, the critic is no longer a godlike voyeur, but rather someone whose subjectivity is implicated in the 'historically and culturally specific knowledges' that she or he produces from work with audience 'informants'.[8] Called interpretive ethnography, this approach records interactions between researchers and informants and places them within their historically specific cultural contexts. This ethnographer can explicate the historical situation of *Miami Vice* and the desires registered by tapping feet.

Neither question raised by the *Miami Vice* presentation, however, can be fully answered by cultural studies methodologies such as those described by Ien Ang. While these approaches have tremendous critical and political value, they do not set out to make manifest or reproduce either the knowledge effects or pleasures of electronic media. The forms of argument employed by media critics are shaped necessarily by the conventions of conceptual analysis. In this vertical or hierarchical model, arguments are built: details are used to support points, and points then support an overarching thesis. The aspect of electronic media that eludes analysis of this sort is precisely its superficiality, its horizontal linkage of images, stories, ads, music, news, soap opera, comedy in a stream of endless contiguities. Pointless (there is no stopping point) transmission and flow replace thesis as an organizing principle. Repetition, rather than the singularity of a well-articulated and argued idea, structures this flow. How can the knowledge effects of electronic media be reproduced or theorized in an idiom appropriate to their form? Gregg Ulmer sees this question as crucial for postmodernist critics: 'The task of post-criticism . . . is to think the consequences for critical representation of the new mechanical means of reproduction (film and magnetic tape . . .).'[9] He finds the means for such 'critical representation' in Jacques Derrida's use of superimposition and mimicry. In constructing a critical work that mimes its object, Derrida evokes text as 'texture' – 'touching' language . . . [that] traces the surface of the object of study . . .'[10] Repetition and textual mime provide knowledge of an object that 'may be obtained without conceptualization or explanation.'[11] While Derrida's objects of study, drawn from philosophy and literature, are very different from the object that concerns me here, his theorizing by mimicry provides a possible model for approaching the media, its knowledge effects,

'Any similarity between persons and events depicted in this book and real persons and events is not only purely coincidental, it's ridiculous.' [*Sex*].

and its pleasures.[12] What might such an essay look or sound like? Patterned on televisual flow, such an argument might draw from an array of academic and popular sources, blatantly mixing the erudite and the mundane. It might abruptly shift discursive registers or genres (changing channels) without any logical justification or articulated transition to rationalize the shift. Ideas would be shaped by allusion, by contiguous arrangement, by a horizontal and superficial logic.

Accordingly, I have invoked my subject by acrostics. I have talked around 'her,' have drawn together a varied array of evidence and details, have tried to switch channels. But as my essay amply demonstrates, avoiding conceptual analysis entirely is not possible nor perhaps desirable. If pressed for a concrete example of a successful theorization of the media, I might look no farther than my subject here. In a sense, the material girl is a theory of electronic media, performed. Allusive (she mimics many of the media icons that have preceded her – Dietrich, Monroe) and eclectic (the texts she imitates range from *Metropolis*, arguably a work with pretensions to high culture, to sixties *Playboy* centrefolds, soft-porn), her textuality crosses genders and genres with aplomb and enacts identity as flow. Pointless, endless and continuously referenced, 'she' becomes all commentary addressed to her: it is her material. The collective ambivalence with which academic critics have approached the media girl bears mention here. Both the fascination and the disgust seem warranted, for this subject seems both to invite and yet not be able to bear the weight of theorization committed to apprehending her. One possibility for future essays might be to alter the subject: instead of using theory to understand Madonna, use Madonna as a model for writing theory differently. The tactics that comprise her – the multiple allusions, genres, sexualities and intertextualities out of which her identity is collaged – and the commentary addressed to her, are far more interesting subjects than she is.

Notes and References

Introduction

1   Madonna has been the subject of frequently sensationalist or idolising publications such as Voller, Debbi, *Madonna: The Style Book*; Omnibus, 1992; or *Madonna: Her Complete Story* David Jones, Publications International, 1991.

2   'Difference' was at the same time the basis for semiotic and structuralist approaches to society. These 'science of signs' methods placed the emphasis in language (Saussure) or visual culture (Barthes). They stressed not the concept which was being expressed but the way it was done, in order to show the underlying bias of a society or individual. The significance of a 'sign' is therefore only in relation to other signs in the chosen system; it is marked by difference.

3   For further discussion of feminist approaches see Kaplan, E. Ann, *Feminist Criticism and Television* in Allen, Robert C, *Channels of Discourse, Reassembled*, University of Carolina Press, 1992 edition.

4   See McQuigan, Jim, *Cultural Populism*, Routledge, 1992, for a clear precis of these ideas.

5   Parker, Rozsika, and Pollock, Griselda, 'Fifteen years of feminist action', *Framing Feminism: Art and the Women's Movement 1970–1985*, Pandora, 1987.

6   Mulvey, Laura, 'Visual Pleasure and Narrative Cinema', *Screen*, Vol. 16, No. 3, 1975, pp. 6–18.

7   Most influential in dismantling or decentering the autonomous individual subject were the French writers: Roland Barthes, *Image-Music-Text*, Fontana, 1977, and Michel Foucault, *The Order of Things*, Tavistock, 1970.

8   Kaplan, p. 264.

9   See Kaplan, E. Ann, (ed.) *Postmodernism and its Discontents; Theories, Practices*, Verso, 1989.

10 Foster, Hal, *Recodings, Art, Spectacle, Cultural Politics*, Bay Press, 1985. Jameson, Fredric, 'Postmodernism, or The Cultural Logic of Late Capitalism', *New Left Review*, 146, July–August 1984. Lyotard, Jean-Francois, *The Postmodern Condition*, Manchester U.P., 1985.

11 The French writer Jean Baudrillard was most extreme in his presentation of the postmodern as 'simulation', the spectacle and a loss of the 'real'. *Simulation*, Semiotext, 1983.

12 For an interesting discussion of this see the 'Introduction' in Epstein, Julia and Straub, Kristina, *Body Guards: The Cultural Politics of Gender Ambiguity*, Routledge, 1991.

13 Madonna's current film, *Body of Evidence*, 1993, directed by Uli Edel, has fuelled this debate. The sex scenes involving sadomasochistic practices, masturbation or explicit body close-ups were drastically cut in America.

Chapter 1

1 Early in 1993, some critics used Madonna's film career to argue that her bubble was about to burst, claiming that she had no acting talent: e.g. Parry, R.L., 'A Material Girl Frays', *The Sunday Times*, 17 January 1993, section 8, p. 9. (This underlines my argument that Madonna is, basically, a musician).

2 *Smash Hits*, Vol. 12, No. 9, 31 October 1990, p. 53.

3 *Observer* magazine, 11 October 1992, p. 37.

4 See e.g. Radway, J., *Reading the Romance*, Chapel Hill: University of North Carolina Press, 1984; Verso, 1987; Radstone, S., (ed.), *Sweet Dreams: Sexuality, Gender and Popular Fiction*, Lawrence and Wishart, 1989.

5 Greig, C., *Will You Still Love Me Tomorrow? The Story of Girl Groups in Pop*, Verso, 1989; see also Wallace, L., (ed.), *The Adoring Audience: Fan Culture and the Popular Media*, Routledge, 1992.

6 For musical as well as cultural analyses see Durant, A., *Conditions of Music*, Macmillan, 1984; Hatch, D. and Millward, S., *From Blues to Rock*, Manchester University Press, 1987; Middleton, R., *Studying Popular Music*, Open University Press, 1990; Blake, A., *The Music Business*, Batsford, 1992.

7 Barthes, R., *Image-Music-Text*, ed. Heath, S., Fontana, 1977.

8 The arrival of psychoanalysis within literary and film theory is narrated in Lapsley, R. and Westlake, M., *Film Theory: an Introduction*, Manchester University Press, 1988. For an overview of this process within feminist theory, and a contestation of some of the counter-arguments see Rose, J., 'Femininity and its Discontents', *Feminist Review*, No. 14, Summer 1983, pp. 5–21.

9 Kristeva's position is summarized and commented on in Coward, R., *Female Desire*, Paladin, 1984; and Moi, T., *Sexual/Textual Politics: Feminist Literary Theory*, Methuen, 1985.

10 Madonna is not alone in this continuity of appeal. In a 1993 survey of 30 students taking a module in popular music studies at the University of East London, 11 claimed the Rolling Stones as a major musical influence. The average age of these eleven was 23: none was born when the Stones had their first chart success.

Chapter 2

1 Spark, Muriel, *The Girls of Slender Means*, London, 1963.

2 Mailer, Norman, *Marilyn*, New York, 1973.

3 See especially Schwichtenberg, Cathy, (ed.), *The Madonna Connection: Representational Politics, Subcultural Identities and Cultural Theory*, Westview Press, 1993.

4 Ibid., p. 57. The essay 'Images of Race and Religion in Madonna's Video "Like a Prayer": Prayer and Praise' was written by Ronald B. Scott.

5 Parker, Dorothy, *The Big Blonde*, p. 187, *The Penguin Dorothy Parker*, Penguin, 1981.

6 O'Brien, Glenn, 'Madonna!', *Interview Magazine*, June 1990.

7 *Independent on Sunday*, 17 January 1993. Paglia interviewed by Zoe Heller.

8 Ibid.

9 Medved, Michael, *Hollywood Vs. America – Popular Culture and the War on Traditional Values*, London, 1993, p. 101.

10 Ibid., p. 97.

11 Bloom, Allan, *The Closing of the American Mind*, New York, 1987, p. 75.

12 Kristol, Irving, 'The Future of American Jewry', *Commentary*, August 1991, p. 25.

13 Pat Buchanan, quoted in the *New York Times*, 15 July 1992.

Chapter 3

1 See Fiske, J., 'British Cultural Studies and Television', in Allen, Robert C., (ed.), *Channels of Discourse*, University of North Carolina Press, 1987. Rowley, Jane, 'Young Women's Responses to Madonna', Unpublished M. Phil, 1992. Schulze, L., White, A.B. and Brown, J., 'A Sacred Monster in Her Prime' in Schwichtenberg, Cathy, (ed.), *The Madonna Connection: Representational Politics, Subcultural Identities, and Cultural Theory*, Westview Press, 1993, pp. 15–33.

2 Her music had previously been popular in dance clubs with both white and black and gay audiences, especially her first album *Madonna*, 1983.

3 Schwichtenberg, p. 134.

4 Kaplan, E. Ann, *Rocking Around the Clock*, Methuen, 1987, pp. 120–123.

5 This does not deny the possibility of other gazes but that they are deliberately constructed around the male.

6 Kaplan, p. 157.

7 Kaplan reads this as a 'daring critique . . . of porn parlours' and Madonna's final androgynous clothing as supporting this subversion of patriarchy. Ibid.

8 See Faludi, Susan, *Backlash: The Undeclared War Against American Women*, Crown Publishers, 1991.

9 Kaplan, p. 117.

10 Tetzlaff, David, 'Metatextual Girl', in Schwichtenberg, p. 250.

11 For the complex arguments that surround body image see Schulze, Laurie, 'On the Muscle' in Gaines, Jane, and Herzog, Charlotte, (eds) *Fabrications: Costume and the Female Body*, Routledge, 1990.

12 Gross, Michael, 'Classic Madonna', *Vanity Fair*, December 1986. *Rolling Stone*, 'The New Madonna', 5 June 1986.

13 Scott, Ronald, 'Images of Race and Religion in Madonna's Video "Like a Prayer"' in Schwichtenberg, pp. 57–74.

14 Ibid.

15 The powerful American Family Association threatened to advise the public to boycott the company, Italian Roman Catholics threatened to file blasphemy charges against them and the record company and Pepsi Cola clearly realized the song could not be separated in the public domain from the video.

16 Quoted by Garber, Marjorie, in *Vested Interests: Cross-Dressing and Cultural Anxiety* (London, Routledge 1992), p. 260.

17 Yule, Paul, *Damned in the USA*, documentary on censorship, 1993.

18 'Voguing' with its excessive feminine masquerade, was originally developed as an aggressive staking of claims to both gay identity and ethnic identity through inter-racial rivalry. See Patton, Cindy, 'Embodying Subaltern Memory', in Schwichtenberg, pp. 91–94.

19 Andersen, Christopher, *Madonna Unauthorized*, Signet, 1991, p. 327.

20 Andrew Neil Interview, Part 2, *The Sunday Times Magazine*, 25 October 1992.

21 The parallels between Koons and Madonna extend further. Koons' themes include race, religion, stardom and sex. He is renowned for self-advertising, exploiting the media and pronouncing his views on personal power, ambition and empowering his audience. Koons, Jeff *The Jeff Koons Handbook*, Thames & Hudson, 1992.

22 Appointing her own art adviser in 1989, Madonna has an extensive art collection and has been listed as one of the 'Top 100' collectors in America. She provided funding for the current Jean-Michael Basquiat Exhibition which opened at the Whitney Museum, New York and will tour America until January 1994. Madonna knew Basquiat and Keith Haring (whose death she laments in *In Bed With Madonna*) from her early days in New York.

23 She references Greta Garbo in her bereted, suited look in Channel 4's *Jonathan Ross Interview*, 1992 and Marlene Dietrich in Jana Lynne Interview, 'The New Music', ITV 23 January 1993.

24 Ibid.

25 Madonna's relationship with Sandra Bernhard established a lesbian identity at a time when her work seemed to raise the issue of diverse sexualities: much later Madonna publicly denied it. Is it because lesbianiam is a threat to Madonna's 'image' which, despite posturing around the choosing of sexualities – is still predicated on luring the male and controlling him without losing her femininity?

26 Schwichtenberg, p. 132.

Chapter 4

1 My work on this paper owes a great deal to Kathleen McHugh's thoughtful advice. I am indebted also to Helen Ogilvy and Tim Thornicroft for help with the latter stages of writing.

2 Although Madonna was given this name by her parents, the decision

to use it alone without her surname has in effect turned it into a stage name.

3   Jung, C.G., 'On the Psychology of the Trickster-Figure', in *The Archetypes and the Collective Unconscious, The Collected Works*, Vol. 9, 1, 2nd ed., Routledge & Kegan Paul, 1968, pp. 255–72.

4   Jung, *The Archetypes and the Collective Unconscious*, p. 48.

5   Jung, 'On the Psychology of the Trickster-Figure', pp. 255–60.

6   Ibid., p. 262.

7   Jung, G.G., *Alchemical Studies, The Collected Works*, Vol. 13, Routledge & Kegan Paul, 1983, pp. 230–4.

8   Jung, *The Archetypes and the Collective Unconscious*, pp. 266, 271–2.

9   Ibid., pp. 265–7; Andrew Samuels, *Jung and the Post-Jungians*, Routledge, 1990, p. 270.

10 Gimbutas, Marija, *The Language of the Goddess*, Harper & Row, 1989, pp. xvii–xx.

11 Gimbutas, pp. 318–9; Jean Shinoda Bolen, *Goddesses in Everywoman: A New Psychology of Women*, Harper & Row, 1985, pp. 20–1.

12 Jacoby, Mario, 'The Witch in Dreams, Complexes, and Fairy Tales: The Dark Feminine in Psychotherapy', in Jacoby, Mario, Kast, Verena, and Riedel, Ingrid, *Witches, Ogres, and the Devil's Daughter: Encounters with Evil in Fairy Tales*, Shambala, 1992, pp. 201–4.

13 Bolen, pp. 199–203.

14 Ibid., pp. 142–3.

15 Ibid., 110–3.

16 Ibid., pp. 78–88.

17 See Tetzlaff, David, 'Metatextual Girl', in Cathy Schwichtenberg (ed.), *The Madonna Connection: Representational Politics, Subcultural Identities, and Cultural Theory*, Westview Press, 1993, pp. 258, 261.

18 Bolen, pp. 82, 92–3.

19 Ibid., pp. 49–50, 60.

20 Ibid., pp. 238–41, 255.

21 Pribram, E. Deidre, 'Seduction, Control, & the Search for Authenticity: Madonna's *Truth or Dare*', in Schwichtenberg, p. 202; Tetzlaff, pp. 255–6.

22 Tetzlaff, p. 259.

23 Henderson, Lisa, 'Justify Our Love: Madonna & the Politics of Queer Sex', in Schwichtenberg, p. 121.

24 Schwichtenberg, pp. 134–5.

25 Pribram, p. 198.

26 Tetzlaff, p. 252.

27 Bordo, Susan, ' "Material Girl": The Effacements of Postmodern Culture', in Schwichtenberg, pp. 285–6.

28 Kaplan, E. Ann, 'Madonna Politics: Perversion, Repression, or Subversion? Or Masks and/as Master-y', in Schwichtenberg, p. 162.

29 Jung, 'On the Psychology of the Trickster-Figure', p. 256.
30 Anthony, Maggy, *The Valkyries: The Women Around Jung*, Element Books, 1990, p.99.

Chapter 5
1   In interview with Simon Bates, BBC Radio One, England, 30 December 1992.
2   Elias, N., *Power and Civility*, Panther Books, 1982.
3   Lees, S., *Losing Out: Sexuality and Adolescent Girls*, Penguin, 1993.
4   Griffin, C., *Typical Girls*, Routledge, 1985.
5   Shepherd, J., *Music as Social Text*, Polity, 1991.
6   McClary, S., *Feminine Endings: Music, Gender and Sexuality*, University of Minnesota Press, 1991.
7   McKinnon, C.A., 'Desire and Power: a feminist perspective', in Nelson, C. and Grossberg, L. (eds), *Marxism and the Interpretation of Culture*, Macmillan, 1988, pp. 105–107.
8   Jeffreys, S., *Anticlimax: a feminist perspective on the sexual revolution*, The Women's Press, 1990.
9   Willis, E., 'Responses to paper by Catherine McKinnon', in Nelson, C. and Grossberg, L. (eds), *Marxism and the Interpretation of Culture*, Macmillan, 1988, pp. 117–121.
10 Stacey, J., 'Desperately Seeking Difference', in Gamman, L. and Marshment, M. (eds), *The Female Gaze: Women as Viewers of Popular Culture*, The Women's Press, 1988, pp. 112–130.
11 Ibid.
12 Vance, C. (ed.) *Pleasure and Danger: Exploring Female Sexuality*, Routledge & Kegan Paul, 1984.
13 Rowley, J., *Young Women's Responses to Madonna: A case study*, unpublished MA thesis, York University.
14 McClary, S., op. cit.
15 Butler, J., *Gender Trouble: Feminism and the Subversion of Identity*, Routledge, 1990.
16 Williams, L., *Hard Core: Power, Pleasure and the 'Frenzy of the Visible'*, Pandora, 1990.
17 Fisher, C., 'Head Girl', *New Musical Express*, 22 June 1991, pp. 18–19 and 44.
18 Reynolds, S., *Blissed Out: the raptures of Rock*, Serpent's Tail, 1990.
19 Williamson, J., 'What men miss about Madonna', *Guardian*, 2 August 1990.
20 Heath, S., 'Joan Riviere and the Masquerade', in Burgin, V., Donald, J. and Kaplan, C. (eds), *Formations of Fantasy*, Methuen, 1986.
21 Walkerdine, V., 'Femininity as Performance', *Oxford Review of Education*, 1989, Vol. 15, No. 3, pp. 267–279.
22 Butler, J., op. cit.
23 Skeggs, B., 'Challenging Masculinity and Using Sexuality', *British Journal of Sociology of Education*, Vol. 12, No. 1, pp. 343–358.

Chapter 6

1 Baudrillard, Jean, *Seduction* (translated by Brian Singer), Macmillan, 1990, p. 8.

2 *Dick Tracy*, directed by Warren Beatty, Touchstone Pictures, 1990.

3 Slam Bradley starred in the early issues of *Detective Comics* (later to feature Batman). He was the work of Jerry Siegel and Joe Shuster – the partnership that created Superman. Rip Kirby was originally created for the newspaper strips by Flash Gordon artist Alex Raymond.

4 Harvey Comics published Dick Tracy comic books from 1942 to 1957. In mint condition these are expensive. Prices are lower in the USA. Blackthorne and Gladstone comics have both published extensive reprints from both the weekly and monthly Dick Tracy stories of the thirties onwards. *See* Overstreet, Robert M., *The Overstreet Comic Book Price Guide*, Avon Books, 23rd Edition, 1993, for a full bibliography of Tracy comics.

5 Madonna, *I'm Breathless: Music from and inspired by the film Dick Tracy*, Sire Records, 1990.

6 For further information on the Warren Beatty/Madonna relationship see, for example, Cahill, Marie, *Madonna*, Omnibus Press, 1991, pp. 78–83.

Chapter 7

I am indebted to Luke Hockley for providing many of the newspaper articles on which this research is based and to Jane Williams for valuable criticism and advice.

1 Madonna, *Sex*, Martin Secker and Warburg, 1992.

2 Baistow, Tom, *Fourth-Rate Estate: An Anatomy of Fleet Street*, Comedia, 1985, p. 45. For a lively account of the tabloid reporting of celebrities see Taylor, S.J., *Shock! Horror! The Tabloids in Action*, Black Swan, 1992, pp. 129–181.

3 Tunstall, Jeremy, *The Media in Britain*, Constable, 1983, p. 76.

4 Antonowicz, Anton, 'A toe job? It's wonderful, er . . . as long as they're clean', *Daily Mirror*, 14 October 1992, p. 16.

5 Katz, Ian, 'Unclad icon screened by wall of hype', *The Guardian*, 9 October 1992, p. 8.

6 Bamigboye, Baz, 'At play in the palace of the material girl', *Daily Mail*, 17 October 1992, pp. 17–18.

7 Kelly, Fergus, Midgley, Dominic, Penman, Andrew and Foyster, Robyn, 'Aren't you sick of Madonna?', *Today*, 14 October 1992, pp. 20–21.

8 Hall, Allan, 'What a thrash', *The Sun*, 17 October 1992, p. 9.

9 Parsons, Tony, 'Cynical star who gives tolerance a bad name', *Daily Telegraph*, 17 October 1992, p. 18.

10 Carpenter, Teresa, 'What's it like being "Mom" to Madonna?', *The Independent*, 12 October 1992, p. 14.

11 Moore, Suzanne, 'Sex and the star', *The Guardian* (Section 2), 21

October 1992, pp. 8–9.

12 For some theories and criticisms of stardom as manipulation see Dyer, Richard, *Stars*, British Film Institute, 1986, pp. 12–16.

13 Amis, Martin, 'Madonna Exposed', *Observer Magazine*, 11 October 1992, p. 36.

14 Bamigboye, 'At play in the palace of the material girl'.

15 Williams, Linda, *Hard Core: Power, Pleasure, and the 'Frenzy of the Visible'*, Pandora, 1990, p. 6.

16 Morgan, Piers, 'The Obscener', *The Sun*, 10 October 1992, p. 9.

17 Gee, Jack, 'Madonna: my book isn't porn', *Daily Express*, 12 October 1992, p. 1. Emphasis added.

18 Braidwood, Philippa, 'Tacky, tawdry and not fit for the children', *Daily Express*, 22 October 1992, p. 5. Emphasis added.

19 Jacques, Jan, and Edwards, Sarah, 'Madonna fun or filth? What the women say about *Sex*', *The Sun*, 22 October 1992, p. 21.

20 Walton, Anthony, and McCashin, Chris, 'Sex with Madonna will put a smile on your face', *Daily Star*, 22 October 1992, p. 5.

21 Gordon, Jane, 'Why men are scared of Madonna', *Today*, 14 October 1992, p. 7.

22 Warner, Marina, 'Body Politic', *The Observer*, 18 October 1992, p. 60. Moore, 'Sex and the star'.

23 Farrel, Nicholas, 'Has material girl got the right stuff?', *The Sunday Telegraph*, 18 October 1992, p.17.

24 For some elaboration on the politics behind this thinking cf. David, Mirian, 'Moral and maternal: the family in the Right', in Levitas, Ruth (ed.), *The Ideology of the New Right*, Polity Press, 1986, pp. 136–168.

25 Bushell, Gary, 'Dangerous sex-ploits', *The Sun*, 22 October 1992, p. 24.

26 Callan, Paul, 'Madonna the great debate', *Daily Express*, 12 October 1992, p. 3.

27 Parsons, 'Cynical star who gives tolerance a bad name', p. 18.

28 Connell, Ian, 'Personalities in the popular media', in Dahlgren, Peter and Sparks, Colin (eds) *Journalism and Popular Culture* Sage, 1992, p. 77.

29 Iley, Chrissey, 'She stoops to conquer' *Sunday Times* (Section 1), 2 August 1992, p. 11.

30 Cable, Amanda, and Lazzeri, Antonell, 'A tortured mind', *The Sun*, 22 October 1992, pp. 22–23.

31 Sanders, Deidre, 'Scarred by childhood', *The Sun*, 22 October 1992, p. 24.

32 Antonowicz, Anton, and McIntosh, Fiona, 'Has she gone too far this time?', *Daily Mirror*, 19 October 1992.

33 cf. Orth, Maureen, 'Madonna in Wonderland', *Vanity Fair*, October 1992, p. 164.

34 Madonna quoted in Romance, Laurence, 'Sex and Romance', *The Guardian* (Section 2), 16 October 1992, p. 5.

35   Neil, Andrew, 'I'm on a mission', *The Sunday Times Magazine*, 25 October 1992, p. 61.

36   Armitage, Gary, Dickey, Julienne and Sharples, Sue, *Out of the Gutter: A Survey of the Treatment of Homosexuality by the Press*, Campaign for Press and Broadcasting Freedom, 1987, p. 16.

37   Parsons, 'Cynical star who gives tolerance a bad name'.

38   Amis, 'Madonna Exposed'.

39   Iley, 'She stoops to conquer'.

40   Coulson, Andy, 'Star denies fling with gay Sandra', *The Sun*, 17 October 1992, p. 9. Gallagher, Jim, 'What Next?', *Today*, 17 October 1992, p. 3.

41   Hellicar, Michael, 'She and Sandra give stud Beatty a sex night he will never forget', *Daily Star*, 12 October 1992, p. 17.

42   Williams, *Hard Core*, p. 140.

43   Farrel, 'Has material girl got the right stuff?'.

44   Connell, 'Personalities in the popular media'. p. 82.

45   Ibid.

46   Skinner, Dr Martin, quoted in 'Angel and devil: the two faces of a star', *Today*, 14 October 1992, p. 21.

47   Madonna quoted in Morgan, Piers, 'Madonna talks to *The Sun*', *The Sun*, 14 October 1992, p. 17.

48   Gallagher, 'What Next?'

49   Neil, 'I'm on a mission'.

Chapter 8

1   Madonna, *Sex*, Martin Secker & Warburg, 1992.

2   Tetzlaff, David, 'Metatextual Girl', in Schwichtenberg, Cathy (ed.), *The Madonna Connection: Representational Politics, Subcultural Identities and Cultural Theory*, Westview Press, 1993, pp. 239–263.

3   Tsiantar, Dody & Hammer, Joshua, 'Sex', *Newsweek*, 2 November 1992, p. 46.

4   Ibid.

5   *This is Spinal Tap*, directed by Rob Reiner, 1983.

6   *Newsweek*, p. 47.

7   Ibid., p. 44.

8   Warner, Marina, 'Body Politic', *The Observer*, 18 October 1992, p. 60.

9   *The Face*, Anniversary Special, No. 21, June 1990.

10   Heller, Zoe, 'Kids I tasted the honey', *The Independent on Sunday*, 25 October 1992, p. 26.

11   Beatty, Warren, quote from *In Bed with Madonna*, Propaganda Films, 1991.

12   Adorno, Theodor and Horkheimer, Max, *Dialectic of Enlightenment*, Verso, 1979.

Chapter 9

1   For those who wish to trace out the debate under its different
    headings see Dworkin, Andrea, *On Pornography: Men Possessing
    Women*, Women's Press, 1981; Snitow, Ann, 'Retrenchment Versus
    Transformation: the Politics of the Antipornography Movement', in
    Burstyn, Varda (ed.), *Women Against Censorship*, Douglas &
    McIntyre, 1985; Kappeler, Suzanna, *The Pornography of
    Representation*, Polity Press, 1986; Ross, Andrew, 'The Popularity
    of Pornography, 2' in *No Respect: Intellectuals and Popular
    Culture*, Kendrick, Walter (ed.), *The Secret Museum: Pornography
    in Modern Culture*, Viking, 1987; 'Pornography: Desperately
    Seeking Consensus', *Marxism Today*, July 1990, pp. 22–25.

2   *Representations*, 1991.

3   See for example Staiger, Janet, 'Seeing Stars', in Gledhill, Christine
    (ed.) *Stardom: Industry of Desire*, Routledge, 1991, pp. 3–16.

4   Schreiber, Martin Hugo Maximilian, *Madonna Nudes 1979*,
    Taschen, 1992 np. On the rapidly changing significance of the
    photographic image see Kracauer, Siegfried, 'Photography', *Critical
    Inquiry*, July 1993, Vol. 19, No. 3, pp. 421–436.

5   Nead, Lynda, *The Female Nude: Art, Obscenity and Sexuality*,
    Routledge, 1992, p. 1, pp. 83–91.

6   Ibid., p. 24–5.

7   Bourdieu, Pierre, *Distinction*, Routledge, 1984.

8   Other areas are left out – scatology seems to be situated as beyond
    the realms of the large market pornographic aesthetic. Paedophilia,
    left out in *Sex* itself, was taken up in the photo essay accompanying
    Orth, Maureen, 'Hot Madonna! The Material Girl's Sexual
    (R)evolution', *Vanity Fair*, October 1992, pp. 92–97.

9   See Hunter, Jefferson, *Image and Word*, Harvard, 1987, for an
    analysis of the relationship of text to image. In 'The Rhetoric of the
    Image', Roland Barthes discusses the repression of extra meanings
    by linguistic explanation (*Image-Music-Text*, Farrar, Strauss and
    Giroux, 1977, trans. Stephen Heath pp. 32–51, p. 40). Here I am
    taking the term in a more specialized way to refer to the linking of
    text and image by the unifying sign of the star.

10 See, for example, Mapplethorpe, Robert, *Mapplethorpe Portraits*,
    National Portrait Gallery, 1988. See 'Lisa Lyon, 1980, 1982',
    'Robert Sherman, 1979', 'Ken Moody and Robert Sherman, 1984'.

11 'Untitled, 1987, #179', *Cindy Sherman*, Mazzotta 1990,
    p. 61. See also her use of the codes of aesthetic beauty and
    femininity in 'Untitled', 1988 # 183, 'Untitled', 1989, # 197, #
    205, # 216. A determined reader could read the last one as echoing
    Sherman's 'Untitled Film Still', 1978, # 15, where a girl looks out of
    a window. See *Cindy Sherman*, Mazzotta 1990, p. 22. See also
    'Untitled Film Stills' # 2, # 6, 1977, in *Untitled Film Stills*,
    Jonathan Cape, 1990. Thanks to Susan Jones's unpublished articles
    on Sherman.

12 Dyer, Richard, *Stars*, BFI, 1979, pp. 34–37.
13 Sontag, Susan, *On Photography*, Penguin, 1977, pp. 16–17.

Epilogue
 1 Valuable conversations with John Izod, Carole-Anne Tyler and
    Stephanie Hammer helped me compose this piece.
 2 Morris, Meagham, 'Banality in Cultural Studies', in Patricia
    Mellencamp (ed.), *Logics of Television*, Indiana University Press,
    1990, pp. 14–43.
 3 Derrida, Jacques, *Spurs*, Barbara Harlow (trans), University of
    Chicago Press, 1978, p. 51.
 4 de Certeau, Michel, *The Practice of Everyday Life*, Stephen Rendell
    (trans), University of California Press, 1984, p. 92.
 5 Ibid., p. 93.
 6 Ellis, John, *Visible Fictions*, Routledge and Kegan Paul, 1982,
    p. 163.
 7 Ang, Ien, 'Wanted: Audiences' in *Remote Control: Television,
    Audiences and Cultural Power*, Ellen Seiter *et alia* (ed.), Routledge,
    1989, p. 101.
 8 Ibid., p. 105.
 9 Ulmer, Gregg, 'The Object of Post-Criticism', in Foster, Hal (ed.)
    The Anti-Aesthetic, Bay Press, 1983, p. 91.
10 Ibid., p. 93.
11 Ibid., p. 94.
12 See Ulmer, Greg, *Teletheory*, Routledge, 1989, for an extensive and
    very compelling account of such a project.

FURTHER READING

Anderson, Christopher, *Madonna Unauthorized* (Signet, 1992). A useful
    source for detailed information on Madonna's life and work.
Butler, Judith, *Gender Trouble: Feminism and the Subversion of Identity*
    (Routledge, 1990). An incisive exploration of binary gender identities
    and possible ways to subvert them.
Doane, Mary Ann, *Femmes Fatales: Feminism, Film Theory,
    Psychoanalysis* (Routledge, 1991). A useful introduction to film theory
    and psychoanalysis. Current methods and theories are used to re-think
    gender identities in classic Hollywood films.
Gaines, Jane & Herzog, Charlotte, *Fabrications: Costume and the Female
    Body* (Routledge, 1990). A collection of broad ranging essays covering
    fashion, film, body building and popular culture.
Garber, Majorie, *Vested Interests: Cross-Dressing & Cultural Anxiety*
    (Routledge, 1992). A detailed, historical account of cross-dressing in
    Western society which covers theatre, film, fashion and subcultures.

Gledhill, Christine (ed.) *Stardom: Industry of Desire* (Routledge, 1991). A collection of essays that explore the nature of stardom and how such images are perceived and meanings constructed.

James, David, *Madonna Her Complete Story, an unauthorized Biography* (Publications International, 1991).

Kaplan, E. Ann, *Rocking Around the Clock – Music, Television Postmodernism and Consumer Culture* (Methuen, 1987). A useful set of essays that addresses general issues of mass media viewing and deconstructs particular examples.

Kaplan, E. Ann, ed., *Postmodernism and its Discontents: theories & practice* (Verso, 1989). This provides a clear account of the diverse meanings of postmodernism and the problems it presents for different feminist approaches.

Madonna, *Sex* (Martin Secker & Warburg, 1992). Plus a free CD of *Erotica*!

McClary, Susan, *Feminine Endings: Music, Gender and Sexuality* (University of Minnesota Press, 1991). A cultural study of popular music which concentrates on analysis of sounds, lyrics and gender.

Nead, Lynda, *The Female Nude: Art, Obscenity and Sexuality* (Routledge, 1992). The problems of the nude whether in art, pornography or advertising are discussed in relation to the constantly changing boundaries each historical age constructs.

Schwichtenberg, Cathy (ed.), *The Madonna Connection: Representational Politics, Subcultural Identities, and Cultural Theory* (Westview, 1993). A hefty theoretical approach that uses Madonna as the connecting point of current cultural debates.

Vance, Carol (ed.), *Pleasure and Danger: Exploring Female Sexuality* (Routledge & Kegan Paul, 1984). A wide ranging set of contributions on heterosexual, bi-sexual and lesbian sexuality and pleasures.

Williams, Linda, *Hard Core: Power, Pleasure and the 'Frenzy of the Visible'* (Pandora, 1990). This discusses both the definitions of pornography and what it represents in our culture.

INDEX

AIDS/HIV 15, 45, 62, 85, 105
Amis, Martin 18, 80, 83, 87, 124(n38)
audiences 10, 18, 28, 35, 39, 40, 48, 52, 56, 58, 67, 73, 77, 79, 93, 97, 110, 113–114, 126(n7)

Barthes, Roland 19, 20, 116(n2, n7), 117(n7), 125(n9)
Baudrillard, Jean 74, 116(n11), 122(n1)
Beatty, Warren 74, 77, 79, 87, 88, 96, 122(notes), 124(n11)
Bernhard, Sandra 69, 87, 88, 119(n25)
Blond Ambition Tour 45, 64, 67, 70

Body of Evidence 47, 117(n13)
Bolen, Jean Shinoda 52–55, 121(notes)
'Borderline' 23, 36, 67, 70
'Burning Up' 23, 70
Butler, Judith, 67, 71

capitalism 10, 14
Catholicism/Church 15, 42, 46, 53, 58, 86, 97, 119(n15)
censorship 15, 30, 34, 44, 85, 99, 106
'Cherish' 25, 67, 70
cultural studies 9–10, 11, 19, 20, 113, 114

Derrida, Jacques 114, 126(n3)
desire 35, 36, 57, 58, 67–71, 89, 103
Desperately Seeking Susan 37
Dick Tracy 23, 74–79, 122(notes)
Dietrich, Marlene 45, 94, 116, 119(n23)
difference/other 10–12, 13–14, 43, 47, 61, 116(n2), 121(n10)

Erotica 17, 20, 22, 26, 27, 47, 62, 67, 69, 70, 72, 91
essentialism 12, 20, 62
Express Yourself 43, 56, 67, 70

feminism/t 12–13, 15, 18, 20, 22, 29, 32, 33, 39, 49, 52, 63, 73, 84, 93, 106, 107, 116(n3, n5)
femininity 39, 44, 62, 63, 71, 107, 117(n8), 119(n25), 121(n21), 125(n11)
First Album 22, 23, 24
Foucault, Michel 117(n7)

gay 9, 13, 15, 40, 44, 45, 47, 56, 62, 64, 71, 107 – *see also* sexualities
Gaze/voyeurism 13, 36–39, 40, 44, 62–64, 68–69, 88, 99, 107, 113, 121(n10)
gender issues 13, 39, 43, 44, 51, 62, 63, 72, 116, 117(n4)

'Hanky Panky' 20, 24, 64, 67, 79
Homosexuality 87, 107, 124(n36) – *see also* sexualities

identity 13, 35–47, 72, 116
I'm Breathless 23, 24, 26, 77–79
In Bed with Madonna (Truth or Dare) 30, 32, 45, 56, 96, 119(n22), 124(n11)

Jung, Carl 49–52, 57, 58, 120(notes), 121(n29)
'Justify My Love' 30, 44, 45, 56, 67, 69, 70

Kaplan, E. Ann 13, 37, 39, 40, 58, 116(notes), 120(n28)
Koons, Jeff 46, 119(n21)
Kristeva, Julia 20, 117(n9)

Leonard, Patrick 17, 18, 19, 26
lesbian 9, 13, 15, 39, 40, 43, 45, 56, 62, 64, 67, 69, 87–88, 106, 110, 119(n25) – *see also* sexualities
'Like a Prayer' 24, 25, 26, 30, 31, 56
Like a Virgin 18, 23, 36, 37, 40, 46, 56, 79
'Lucky Star' 36

Mapplethorpe, Robert 44, 46, 64, 91, 107, 125(n10)
Marxism 12, 40, 121
masculinities 63, 69, 72, 93, 121(n23)

masquerade 47, 56, 71–73, 119(n18), 121(n20)
'Material Girl' 36, 37
Meisel, Steven 95, 105
Monroe, Marilyn 30, 32, 33, 37, 45, 71, 89, 96, 101, 116, 117(n2)
M.T.V., 31, 37, 44
Mulvey, Laura 62, 117(n6)
music 9, 10, 17–28, 62, 65, 67, 69

Nead, Lynda 101, 103, 125(n5)
Neil, Andrew 80, 87, 89, 119(n20), 124(n35, n49)
New Right 14, 33, 85, 123(n24)

'O Father' 25, 45, 65
'Open Your Heart' 37, 39, 68

'Papa Don't Preach' 67
patriarchy 12, 13, 14, 15, 20, 22, 40, 43, 45, 46, 53, 69, 118(n9)
pleasure 13, 19, 20, 22, 27, 47, 48, 62, 64, 68, 70, 105, 106, 110, 114
pornography 46, 62, 67–69, 83–84, 90, 99, 100–103, 105, 106, 108, 126(n1)
postmodernism 9, 13–14, 15, 17, 27, 29, 31, 43, 44, 46, 48, 56, 72, 91, 114
power 37, 39, 47, 48, 52, 57, 59, 67, 69, 72, 99

race 9, 32, 34, 39, 40, 42, 43, 48, 63, 97
religion 30, 35, 42, 43, 48, 53, 58, 59
Rogers, Nile 18, 19, 23

sadomasochism/S&M 15, 20, 43, 44, 47, 64, 65, 71, 79, 86, 96, 97, 106, 117(n13)
Schreiber, Martin 100–103
Schwichtenberg, Cathy 36, 117(n3), 119(notes), 120(notes), 121(notes), 125(n2)
Scott, Ronald 118(n4), 119(n13)
semiotics 15, 20, 99, 113, 116(n2)
Sex 29, 33, 46, 64, 65, 71, 80–90, 91–98, 99–100, 103–110, 124(n1)
sexuality/ies 15, 26, 30, 35, 39, 43, 44, 46, 56, 57, 58, 61–64, 67, 69, 71–73, 79, 86, 93 – *see also* gay/lesbian
Sherman, Cindy 46, 107, 125(n11)
signs 13, 14, 15, 43, 44, 45, 99, 116(n2)

Tetzlaff, David 40, 55, 56, 93, 118(n10), 120(notes), 124(n2)
'Till Death Us Do Part' 25, 65
True Blue 20
2 Live Crew 34, 45

'Vogue' 24, 26, 45, 67, 79
Voguing 120(n18)

'Waiting For You' 26, 27